HIS
IMAGE
MY
IMAGE

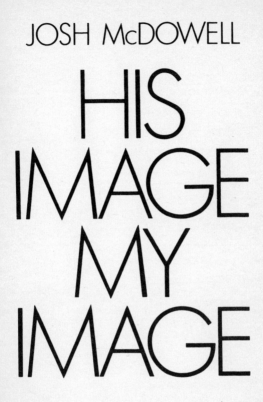

JOSH McDOWELL

HIS IMAGE MY IMAGE

CAMPUS CRUSADE FOR CHRIST

Published by
SCRIPTURE PRESS FOUNDATION (UK) LTD
Amersham-on-the-Hill, Bucks, England

For more information about the
Ministry of Campus Crusade
for Christ, write to:

England: Campus Crusade for Christ—103 Friar Street,
Reading RG1 1EP, Berkshire
Australia: L.I.F.E.—P.O. Box A399, Sydney South 2000
Canada: Campus Crusade for Christ of Canada—Box 368,
Abbottsford, B.C, V25 4N9
New Zealand: Lay Institute for Evangelism—P.O. Box 8786, Auckland 3
West Africa: Great Commission Movement of Nigeria—P.O. Box 500,
Jos, Plateau State. Nigeria
Republic of South Africa: Life Ministry—P.O. Box/Bus 91015,
Auckland Park 2006
USA: Campus Crusade for Christ International—Arrowhead Springs,
San Bernardino, CA 92414
Ireland: Campus Crusade for Christ—264 Merrion Road, Dublin 4

To

MARY CROWLEY

A cherished friend whose positive self-image is
very contagious.

Acknowledgements

It is with deep gratitude and appreciation that I acknowledge
the contribution of the following people to this manuscript:
Waylon Ward for his extensive psychological research and
counsel, Marty Williams for putting the notes into written
form, Dick Day for his wise counsel and personal insights,
Dr Lawrence J. Crabb Jr for reviewing the manuscript and
doing the Foreword and Dr Robert Saucy for reading
through the material from a theological viewpoint.

Contents

Preface

If you can think of anyone you would rather be than yourself, you probably have a self-image problem.

One student came up to me at a university and said, 'Josh, I know at least twenty people I'd rather be than myself.' Perhaps this response is true of you.

How would you answer these two questions?

1. What are you worth as a person? Not, what are the chemicals in your physical body worth, but what are *you* worth?

2. Are you happy (or excited) about who you are?

The way you answer these questions may play a key role in how you live your life, in the joy you experience, in the way you treat others and in how you respond to God. It isn't who you are so much as who you think you are that determines these life responses.

Perhaps the consideration of such questions is new to you. Maybe you've never realized that people have true value, that we all are made in the image of the Creator and are 'crowned with honour and glory,' as Psalm 8:4 and 5 declares us to be.

Maybe you believe, as behaviourists do, that life is just a cosmic accident in a vast galaxy, and people are programmed machines. Maybe you believe, as existentialists do, that we are an absurdity—or, as humanistic evolutionists do, that we are only animals whose genetic ancestry goes back to the ape.

On the other hand, many people today like to believe that man is totally independent and autonomous. They claim that science and technology have pushed back barriers that formerly constrained us, that we are no longer tied to our ancestors' old superstitions and fears and that we are free to live life any way we choose.

Rather than being set free to realize our full potential, though, many people today are more apt to have to come to grips with a different problem, that of finding personal significance of some sort while at the same time relating to a universe that is greater than any they ever knew existed before. If we see man as only an inconsequential speck in the universe, it's easy to feel that the whole area of personal value and significance is extremely tenuous. As a result, people are hurting emotionally and crying out for help.

They're like a fellow named Jeff, who wrote to me to say, 'I'm writing because I'm alone and confused. I just don't feel that my life is worth living any more. I cry myself to sleep every night. Sometimes I just wish I were dead.'

Jodi Foster (the actress who was the object of John Hinckley's distorted love and the motivation for his shooting President Reagan) has revealed a similar problem that an actress friend of hers has. In an interview, Jodi said, 'The funniest part about my friend is that she is one of the prettiest girls in the world, but she think's she's incredibly ugly; she considers herself grotesque. That's why she can't trust anyone who says they love her. It's like, "God, if You love me, You must be a real fool."'

The only reality to this girl's viewpoint is that God does love her. The error in her thinking is her failure to realize that, since God is her Creator, only He can give an accurate estimation of her worth and value. Only He can realistically answer her longings for acceptance and love.

People still need to know that they are loved and have

worth. Rather than being outdated, this is where Christianity speaks to modern people's needs in a unique way. A personal relationship with Jesus Christ sets an individual free to be all that he or she was created to be.

When people respond to Christ, they don't just embrace a philosophy of life. They establish a unique personal relationship with their Creator. It's a union that makes it possible for them not only to have an increased sense of self-worth but also to do things of lasting value. Christians can know that the God of the universe accepts and loves them. They can begin to see themselves as children of the King and then start acting like just that—Christian royalty. Let me explain what I mean.

Each person has special importance as God's creation. When God moves into a person's life, that person's value becomes infinite, eternal and unchanging because of the One who lives within.

The need today for people to know that they are loved and are significant is critical. As we move closer to the twenty-first century, society around us may increasingly communicate a message that personal significance is exactly the opposite of what we have. Rather than feeling loved and having worth, it will be even easier for us to feel that we are isolated, emotionally cut off from others or being used by others, and are just another cog in the machine.

This book has been written to help you understand God's perspective of you. From experience, I know that a proper biblical view of God, of yourself, and of others can be a liberating force in your life. You are not alone in your struggle for identity. Your hurts and heartaches have been shared by many others, including myself. Even though the struggle can be difficult and the healing process draining, when you seek to find your self-image in God's image of you, the struggle is worth it.

As you begin to apply the principles in this book, and to see yourself as God sees you, my prayer is that the resulting healing and transforming that occurs will allow you to start acting out a godly image of yourself in every aspect of your life.

Foreword

Every culture has its own unique and absorbing concerns. In the world of struggling, growing Christians, the issue of self-esteem has occupied the centre stage for several years and shows no signs of soon yielding the spotlight.

The questions people ask about self-esteem are both many and important. For example, is a Christian supposed to work at building a positive self-image? Or do such efforts lead us further into the morass of self-preoccupation and further away from pressing on for Christ?

Is our modern concern for self-image really a trojan horse smuggling secular values into the Christian church? Are weightier matters like holiness, obedience and personal sacrifice receiving too little attention as counsellors encourage us to 'find ourselves' and to 'affirm our value'?

Or is a healthy self-image an intended blessing of knowing the Lord? Is there not a legitimate healing of many internal wounds as one grows in understanding of who Christ is and what He has done? Perhaps that healing is felt as an improved self-concept. Maybe spiritual growth involves a deepening awareness of one's own dignity and purpose.

Questions about one's self-image won't go away—and they shouldn't. They are important, especially to the thousands of people who are honest enough to admit that something is missing in their Christian experience. More people than we suspect live in private despair, wondering if anyone really cares, struggling to believe that what they do matters to someone.

Too often, responses to these problems amount to little more than shallow affirmations about one's value and worth which comfortably overlook the reality of man's sinfulness, a problem which justifies a realistically negative self-appraisal.

On the other hand, people who accept the biblical position about sin sometimes offer harshly simplistic solutions to the problem of self-esteem such as, 'Stop fussing about yourself and get on with living as you should,' or, 'Just believe what God says, then learn it, pray and witness.'

Josh McDowell has written a much-needed, balanced discussion of self-esteem, compromising neither the ugly truth of human depravity or the exhilarating truth of human dignity. His treatment of this topic reflects a compassionate sensitivity to the very real struggles rumbling inside people who may look happy and content.

As I began reading the book, I wondered if his rich awareness of the pain which a poor self-image can bring would lead Josh to dilute a solid biblical perspective with a 'let's make people feel better quick' position and encouragement to 'like yourself' as a pre-condition for obedience. I was thrilled to find that rare combination of (1) clear commitment to the Word of God and (2) warm insight into where people really live. (How sad that two elements which should always go together rarely do!)

Josh's open sharing of his own struggle with a stubbornly bad self-image stands out to me as the most encouraging part of the book. The reader cannot help but be caught up in the contagious joy of growing into a fuller realization of who we are in Christ and what we can do in His name.

One further thought. This is no academic treatise. Every chapter is filled with real-life illustrations and practical suggestions for biblically dealing with low self-esteem. The balance between theory and practice is just right. Josh has carefully laid the foundations for thinking through the issues surrounding self-esteem and then has brought abstract concepts down to the level where all of us live.

LAWRENCE J. CRABB JR, PH.D.

Introduction

This book can change your life!

As we read a book we often decide to learn principles or passages, do something special for someone or change something in our lives.

All too often, weeks later, we have completely forgotten our good intentions. So here are five practical ways of turning good intentions into practical habits.

1. Obtain some record cards

Write out the principles or passages you want to learn on some record cards. (A convenient size is 5 × 3 inches.) them with you for a month or two. Read these cards whenever waiting for a doctor, the children at school, travelling in the car or before going to sleep at night.

2. Mark your calendar for a major review

Mark your calendar or diary *today* for a time when you will review your good intentions once per month. Don't be discouraged if you don't do everything you've planned... just don't stop.

3. Re-read what you've underlined

Underline key portions of this book, then re-read what you have underlined again and again...not the whole book. Once you have read something ninety times you will have learnt it whether you plan to or not. I'm not suggesting you read the underlining in a book ninety times...but the principle of re-reading helps 'brand the principles into your brains'.

4. Apply the material immediately

There is an old saying:

> Hear something...you forget it
> See something...you remember it
> Do something...you understand it.

Apply what you learn as soon as you possibly can...it helps you understand the material and remember it.

5. Work out priorities in what you want to learn

Ask yourself, 'What one to three things out of this book do I really want to apply faithfully and make a habit?'

Remember, every person alive struggles with turning their good intentions into habits...these are five thoughts from a fellow struggler.

1

Self-Image: What Is It?

Have you ever showed someone the pictures in your wallet? Of course you have. Maybe you were inwardly pleased at how impressed that person was with the photo of someone really special to you. Maybe you let them see a lovely portrait of your mum and dad. Perhaps, if you're older and married, you beamed with pride as your friend ooohed and aaahed over your beautiful children. But when that friend happened to see the photo on your passport, it was a different matter. That shot is too inaccurate for anyone to really grasp. You don't really look like that!

Yet each of us also carries another portrait with us, a picture far more important than any in our wallet. Psychologists have a name for it (don't they have a name for everything?). They call that mental picture of ourselves our *self-image*.

Now a few of you may like the passport picture. And some of us like our inner self-portrait. A lot of us, however, would be embarrassed if our heart opened up like a wallet and someone accidentally saw inside it what we think we look like. Beyond that, there's always the person whose self-image is bent all out of shape, like a photo carried too long in a wallet.

I don't need to tell you that women with pretty faces or men with rugged good looks generally get more attention than those of us with less attractive features (as the world judges them). Similarly, the person with a healthy, positive self-image tends to be out in front in the race of life. Whether we like it or not, our mental self-portrait, that self-image, has a tremendous bearing on our emotional and spiritual well-being. Why is that?

Research has shown that we tend to act in harmony with our mental self-portrait. If we don't like the kind of person we are, we think no one else likes us either. And that influences our social life, our job performance, our relationships with others.

That is why one writer styled the new insights about self-image, 'the most important psychological discovery of this century.' A Christian psychologist says, 'An adequate self-concept [another name for self-image] is a precious possession. . . . An inadequate self-concept is a handicap.'

When did you get your mental portrait of yourself? How was it shaped?

For all of us the foundation begins to be laid the moment the doctor places us in our mother's arms. At that point we start relating to our parents and other members of our family. By the age of five or six our self-concept, the person we think we are in relationship to others, is so firmly established that we will resist efforts to change it.

Can a healthier self-image be developed?

At this point some of you may be saying, 'Oh boy, I've certainly got a bad foundation! No wonder I've got such problems.' Maybe a counsellor has even told you that. As a result you've about given up on any significant change. After all, who can re-lay a foundation?

I am here to tell you that your self-portrait is *not* permanently affixed in place like a photo encased in plastic in your wallet. You can change it. You can develop a more accurate and healthy view of yourself. True, weaknesses, blind spots and natural tendencies may occasionally distort the picture, but, as you learn to see yourself as God sees you, that distortion factor will decrease.

Ever notice what a difference the right lighting can make on a photo, or the distortion a dark shadow creates? The good news of the tremendous worth we have in God's eyes can light up our inner self-portrait. On the other hand, the sin resulting from our sin nature can throw a shadow over that self-image.

Those of you who know me or who have read my biography, *A Sceptic's Quest,* know what a pitiful foundation for a good self-image was laid in my life. If I let those experiences shape my view of myself, I would be overflowing with rage. But because I (1) came to know God personally through Jesus Christ, (2) absorbed the character of God by studying His Word and (3) let other Christians help in reshaping my self-understanding, I now see myself more as Jesus sees me. More and more I like what I see in my self-portrait.

You too can experience that transformation. You can have your self-image reprogrammed through understanding and applying the biblical principles in this book. I want to help you see yourself as God sees you. I want to help you discover who you are, the special individual you have been created to be in the eyes of God (Rom 12:3).

What is meant by self-worth?

What you think of yourself, your self-image or sense of self-worth, influences every part of your life. Other terms closely related to self-worth are self-concept and self-esteem. Although those words don't mean precisely the same thing, they are often used interchangeably.

Our self-image has a definite structure, composed of conclusions we have reached about ourselves. If our parents and grandparents kept saying we were stupid, we began to believe it and to act as if we were. Our marks at school began to reflect our opinion about ourselves.

You may be a young housewife. If you weren't taught the art of cooking and your husband reinforces your feeling that you can't cook as well as his mother did, you may never master the culinary arts. 'Everything I cook turns out a terrible mess,' you may say to yourself and to other people (which of course reinforces your opinion about this skill). Actually you are probably perfectly able to master the art of cooking, but your feeling about your lack of ability prevents you from ever doing well at it. And that lack has its roots in your past as well as in the present.

Though our feelings about ourselves may be deeply rooted in our conscious and subconscious minds, there is hope. Part of our self-image is dynamic and changing. That part grows and evolves through all the interactions of daily life. It is like a fabric that is being woven and stretched over a hard inner frame to form an outer (conscious) sense of who we are.

A friend moved from a town in which people in her church had had a highly critical, perfectionist attitude. During her years there she felt as though she had to prove herself over and over again. Her sense of self-worth had to be constantly reinforced by her husband and children. In her new community she experienced warm accepting attitudes. She quickly found a satisfying involvement in her new church, with considerable affirmation of her value. Her self-image and sense of self-worth improved because she felt she was accepted for who she was, just as God accepted her just as she was.

We sail on a bouncy sea

The hard, inner structure of one's self-image, formed early in life, may be compared to the masts of a great sailing ship. The sails hoisted up the masts are the changing fabric of who you believe you are. The sails ride on the masts and turn with the wind. Your self-image ebbs and flows in daily interactions.

When you receive positive messages from your environment, you ride a strong wind and think well of yourself. You feel good about who you are and what you are doing with your life. Your ship is in full sail. At other times your ship is becalmed by lack of contact or meaningful interaction with friends and loved ones. At still other times you toss and turn, roughed up by angry winds of criticism and accusations from others—or even from yourself.

Sails get torn in life's storms. In a particularly devastating storm—divorce, loss of a job, death of a loved one—some ships crash onto a rocky beach, or a mast snaps. Those ships can be repaired, but the rebuilding is often a long and arduous task.

Most of our masts, however, are adequate for the sails to billow on. They get a sail torn only occasionally.

Persons with a good, healthy sense of self-worth feel significant. They believe that they matter, even that the world is a better place because they are there. Such persons can interact with others and appreciate their worth too. They radiate hope, joy and trust. They are alive to their feelings. They accept themselves as delightful to God—a ship moving forward confidently, under full sail. They believe in themselves as lovable, worthy and competent parts of God's creation, sinful by nature, but redeemed and reconciled to God to become all He wants them to be.

We rob ourselves

An inadequate self-image robs us of the energy and powers of attention to relate to others because we are absorbed with our own inadequacies. That is especially true when we're in the presence of people who remind us of our shortcomings or whose judgement about ourselves we value and want to influence. In such situations we are so self-conscious that we cannot give sufficient attention to others. As a result we may be regarded as being either uncaring or proud. Our feelings of inadequacy prevent us from reaching out to love and care for others.

For example, a student who appears to be very secure wrote to me, 'I think of myself as a misfit. I'm so scared of what people think of me. It's hard to accept myself. I still feel afraid of looking people in the eye or of even being around them. I feel like rubbish. My fear of rejection by others is great.'

Persons with an inadequate self-image look to other people's opinions, praise or criticisms as determining factors in how they feel or think about themselves at a particular moment. Persons with a poor sense of self-worth are slaves to the opinions of others. They are not free to be themselves.

An inadequate self-image
robs us of the energy and
power of attention to relate
to others.

Bob, an attractive person, well dressed, groomed to perfection, walks with an air of confidence that demonstrates the principles he teaches as a motivational speaker. He regularly addresses business groups about motivation, successful sales techniques and personal confidence. He has a firm, confident handshake and other mannerisms that experts say communicate security, success and assertiveness. So what is he doing in a counsellor's office?

As he tells about his mate's rejection of him, his confident façade begins to crack. Marital conflict has caused his underlying feelings of inadequacy to surface. Broken, Bob confesses his fears of failing without his wife's support. The usually buoyant fabric of his self-image has been ripped, revealing the weak inner structure hidden beneath.

Regrettably, many people perceive themselves more according to a picture of themselves formed early in life than by their accomplishments as adults. Many individuals who are outwardly successful are constantly depressed and anxious inside because of the poor self-image they developed in childhood. The façade of their self-image (the sails of their ship) appears to be strong and resilient, but the underlying structure (the masts) are warped and brittle. In crises, that inadequate undergirding of their self-worth becomes evident.

Persons with a poor sense of self-worth expect to be cheated, rejected and deprecated in life. Expecting the worst, they often create what they fear. They engage in self-defeating behaviour, distrust and suspicion. They struggle with the tension of trying to be acceptable while believing they are not.

Take Karen, for instance. As she walked into a counsellor's office, she resembled a stork: tall, lanky and stooped. Her bearing depicted her deep sense of inadequacy and depression. Her clothes spoke of poverty and farm life in the Middle West of the United States. Her behaviour showed that she felt anything but good about herself. She was almost childlike, a frightened waif with eyes that darted about the room.

Everything about Karen said, 'No one could possibly like looking at me. No one would ever consider me important enough to pay attention to.' She had sought out a counsellor because she was sure her husband, a pastor, would have to leave his ministry if she were caught in what had become compulsive habits—shoplifting and, more recently, abusing a child she took care of.

Karen's poor self-image had resulted in an inadequate sense of self-worth. That had contributed to her sinful actions and habits, and these compounded still further her poor view of herself.

Could Karen's self-image and sense of self-worth be altered? Today when you run into Karen you see a significantly different woman: a vibrant pastor's wife, a loving mother of three children of her own.

We look at life through spotty lenses

Your self-image is like a set of lenses through which you view reality. Based on what you see through those lenses, you choose a pattern of behaviour you consider appropriate for a particular situation. If your lenses distort the situation, your behaviour won't fit in with reality. The healthier your self-image, the more accurately your lenses let you see the reality and the more appropriate your behaviour is in response.

It's like the old illustration of a black speck on a white page. Some people see the black speck and focus on it. Others see all the white space and concentrate on that. It depends on one's perspective.

The same is true of the self-worth of a person like Marilyn, an attractive woman in her late twenties. Her posture and tense facial muscles openly advertise her problem. For several years friends have encouraged her to get help to improve her sense of self-worth. Even though she has lots of friends, she is so certain she is unlovable that she refuses to believe that anyone really cares for her.

Marilyn is an example of someone acting in harmony with her self-image. She thinks and behaves in a sexually degrading manner, like the kind of person she sees herself to be. Her limited focus then zooms in still closer on only these demeaning actions of her life—which distorts still further her perception of herself.

If you see yourself as a failure, you will find some way to fail, no matter how hard you want to succeed. On the other hand, if you see yourself as adequate and capable, you will face life with more optimism and perform nearer your best.

Whichever view of yourself you choose to focus on will become a key ingredient to the success and happiness you find in life. John DeVines, author of *How Much Are You Worth?*, summarizes the importance of this. Your view of yourself, he writes, is 'far more important than most people think it is'. He says:

> The answer to how much I am worth determines
> whether I am happy or sad,
> excited or depressed,
> in love with life
> or thinking about suicide.
>
> If I think that I am valuable—worth a lot—
> I will function well at my job,
> get along better with my spouse,
> and have a tremendous sense of well-being.
> But if I think I am worthless,
> I lack motivation for work,
> and am convinced that everything I do will fail.[1]

Building
a better self-image

Take a look at your self-image to see where you stand. Are you satisfied with who you are at this point in your life (assuming that you expect further personal growth in the future)? _____

Do you have (or fight) an inflated view of who you are, when you compare yourself with others? _____

Do you dislike the mental portrait you have of yourself?

_____

List five strong points and five weaknesses you see in yourself.

Strong Points

_____

_____

_____

Weaknesses

_____

_____

_____

Which list of characteristics took you longer to identify?

_____

Does this tell you anything about your self-image?

_____

_____

2

A New Name for a Biblical Concept

Christians who are counsellors and teachers approach psychology from a different perspective than do their secular counterparts. We base our ministry on the presupposition that God cares about His creation, humankind. We believe that from His heart of compassion and love God revealed Himself to humankind, and that everything He has revealed is truth. This revealing or revelation reaches us in two ways.

First, God reveals Himself to us through other parts of His creation. Romans 1:20 tells us that every person has evidence of God's existence through what He has created, which includes all of nature, including the human race. God made Himself known through what He created. Theologians call this 'general revelation'.

The Scriptures also say that God commanded humankind to have dominion, or power to rule, over His creation, to subdue it and be in charge of it (Gen 1:28). That command was responsible for the foundation of science and the scientific method, which psychologists now use to study human beings and their behaviour. Christian counsellors, too, believe that the scientific method is the best system yet devised to study and explore those parts of God's created universe that are not specifically discussed in the Bible.

The second way that God reveals Himself is through the person of Jesus Christ and through the Bible. Theologians call this 'special revelation'. Many secular scientists consider this form of revelation irrelevant or even impossible. But those of us who know God personally, and who are involved in Christian counselling and meeting people's needs from a biblical basis, pay attention to special revelation. We believe that it provides specific knowledge that God wants us to have, knowledge about the 'riddle of life' that is not available through any other source.

We believe that the Bible is the written part of God's special revelation, which He has provided for us as a basis of absolute truth. Through the Bible we can confirm or invalidate what we perceive from our scientific research and our study of general revelation. Without the Bible as a method of validating our discovered truth, we are likely to be left entangled in the ideas and whims of our own minds.

Is this concept biblical?

Is the idea of self-image only a whim of our entangled minds, just another effort to focus selfish attention on ourselves?

If the existence of an individual's self-concept could be established by our five senses—what we see, feel, hear, touch or taste—then its existence could be proven through the scientific method. Self-image, however, is only a term used to explain what we believe about ourselves. Self-image has no concrete existence in itself.

Can a case for the existence of self-image be built from special revelation, the Bible? Is such an idea or concept seen in Scripture? While we don't want to read our psychology into our theology, at the same time we shouldn't be afraid to examine information discovered through psychology to see if it offers help in our search to understand ourselves. It is important to sift our concepts, whether psychological ones or not, through the grid of God's Word.

In chapter one, self-image was defined as what we think

and feel ourselves to be. Once we agree to that understanding of self-image, we can find many passages in both
the Old and New Testaments that indicate that we do think
and have feelings about ourselves. A few of these are:

> Do nothing out of selfish ambition or vain conceit, but in
> humility consider others better than yourselves. Each of you
> should look not only to your own interests, but also to the
> interests of others. Your attitude should be the same as that of
> Christ Jesus.[1]
>
> For through the grace given to me I say to every man among
> you not to think more highly of himself than he ought to think;
> but to think so as to have sound judgment, as God has allotted
> to each a measure of faith.[2]
>
> Since, then, you have been raised with Christ, set your hearts
> on things above, where Christ is seated at the right hand of
> God. Set your minds on things above, not on earthly things.
> For you died, and your life is now hidden with Christ in God.
> When Christ, who is your life, appears, then you also will
> appear with him in glory.... and have put on the new self,
> which is being renewed in knowledge in the image of its Creator.[3]
>
> Finally, brothers, whatever is true, whatever is noble, what-
> ever is right, whatever is pure, whatever is lovely, whatever is
> admirable—if anything is excellent or praiseworthy—think
> about such things.[4]

Many other passages (Rom 12:16; Phil 4:7; Mt 6:25–34;
6:19–21; Jn 13:1–3) can be cited to show the scriptural
recognition that human beings have thoughts and feelings
about themselves, and that these attitudes affect their
behaviour.

Scriptural illustrations of self-image

Today's psychologically oriented writers might be surprised
to learn that the concept of self-image was around long
before the twentieth century. About 3,000 years ago King
Solomon made an acute observation of the relationship

between what a man thinks and how he acts. Solomon wrote: 'As he thinketh in his heart, so is he' (Prov 23:7, AV).

Dr Earl Radmacher gives one of the most descriptive commentaries I've ever read on King Solomon's cogent advice to a man who is about ready to be conned into a bad deal:

> He (King Solomon) portrays a situation in which a rich, prestigious ruler wants to swindle a dinner guest. In order to accomplish the rip-off, the rich man pretends to be sincerely interested in his guest. As soon as he gets what he wants, though, he'll drop him like a hot potato. King Solomon counsels, "Don't go by appearances. Things are not always what they seem to be. A man isn't necessarily what he says or does. His speech and actions may be contrived to fool you. In the final analysis, only what lies deep inside the counsels of a man's heart presents a true picture of what the man is."

You know how this works, don't you? A person can put on a big smile and shake hands with another person, pretending to care, when he really doesn't have two cents worth of interest in the other person. Maybe you have been the other person a time or two, and consequently you have learned not to go just by what you see on the surface. You get the point Solomon makes: "as he thinketh in his heart, so is he."

Let me explain that word *heart*, because it had a different meaning when the Bible was written than it has today. You might tell someone, "I love you with all my heart," but in Bible times you would have said, "I love you will all my kidneys," or "I love you with all my bowels." You see, in Bible times the kidneys and bowels were regarded as the center of human affection, whereas the heart was regarded as the center of reflection. What Solomon was driving at, then, when he advised, "As he thinketh in his heart so is he," is simply this: "As a man thinks in the center of his deepest reflection, that's what he will be." The things he thinks about deeply are the raw materials which form his actions.[5]

Another verse which also reflects that we do indeed have a self-concept is Numbers 13:33. It states, 'There also we saw the Nephilim (the sons of Anak are part of the Nephilim): and we became like grasshoppers in our own sight, and so we were in their sight' (NASB). The spies who were sent out to look at the promised land came back with their report and stated that there were giants in the land, and all but two, Joshua and Caleb, advised staying out, even though the land was rich, as God had promised. The point here is that Joshua and Caleb perceived themselves quite differently from the way the others did.

The majority, when they looked at the giants, saw themselves as only grasshoppers compared to the sons of Anak, and they cowered in fear. The passage indicates that their perception of themselves affected how the enemy saw them as well—they were considered just a group of grasshoppers. The spies' view of themselves affected their perspective on the entire situation.

However, with Joshua and Caleb it is quite clear that they did not regard themselves as grasshoppers. They saw themselves in the light of the presence of God, confident they could claim the land. The fact is they had a realistic appraisal of themselves. They were not haughty, or overly self-confident. They were not as the majority, filled with fear, without confidence, and holding a low opinion of themselves and of God. Rather, they were God-confident —not cocky, but sure of themselves in the Lord, and sure of His promises.

Other passages indicating the reality of a person's self-image, or objective description of oneself, likewise illustrate the concept's validity. Some of these include Cain when his countenance had fallen (Gen 4:5–7), David after Nathan confronted him with his sin (2 Sam 12; Ps 51), Peter's valiant testimony about who Christ was and, soon afterwards, his denial of even knowing Him (Lk 22:33–34, 54–62).

Investigating the lives of the men and women of the Bible to see how their faith was related to self-image can be an exciting study. A good example is the difference between the letters Paul wrote to Titus and those he wrote to Timothy. Various indications in those letters show that Timothy had a weaker self-image than Titus.

With that in mind, we can understand why Paul reminded Timothy of the prophecies made about him when he was ordained (1 Tim 1:18; 4:14), admonishing him to persevere in using his gift of ministering God's Word and not to think (implied), or let others think, that he was any less a minister because of his youth.

Later Paul gave lengthy instructions on how Timothy should relate to the people to whom he was ministering. He reminded him that God didn't give us a 'spirit of timidity' (1 Tim 4—5; compare 2 Tim 1:7).

In his second letter to Timothy, Paul gave much space to encouraging and building Timothy's hope by reminding him of the confidence that he had in him.

In contrast is Paul's letter to Titus. He didn't address Titus as a ministering pastor, but as an apostle, giving him didactic instructions that are straight to the point. There are no personal passages to encourage or build up Titus's faith. Evidently Paul didn't think they were needed.

> *A healthy self-image is*
> *'seeing yourself as God sees*
> *you—no more and no less.'*

Paul referred to the thoughts, beliefs and feelings that individuals are to have towards themselves when he said we each should have the same attitude within ourselves that Christ had (Phil 2:5–16). Paul alluded to his own self-image when he wrote, 'By the grace of God I am what I am.'[6] Another one of Paul's statements is: 'Each one should test his own actions. Then he can take pride in himself, without comparing himself to somebody else.'[7]

So far we have defined self-image as 'what we think and feel ourselves to be.' For a truly biblical definition, let's expand that a bit. A healthy self-image is 'seeing yourself as God sees you—no more and no less.' That definition lies behind my titling this book, *His Image...My Image*. In other words, a healthy self-image means having a realistic view of ourselves from God's perspective, as we are portrayed in His Word. I add the phrase 'no more and no less' because some people have an inflated view of themselves (pride), while others have a self-deprecating view of themselves (false humility). Sometimes this is a result of pride and other times a result of the lack of knowledge. What we need is a realistic and biblical view.

Today's culture strongly dictates an unbiblical view. It often makes statements about humanity that may sound biblical, but that are without any biblical basis. Some of those assertions are incredibly grandiose. From now on, we will assume the above definition of 'healthy-self-image', *seeing ourselves as God sees us—no more and no less*. That way we will have correct biblical, emotional and mental assumptions about ourselves.

Is self-worth biblical?

Many Christians are uneasy about the notion of acknowledging *any* self-worth. They are adamantly against the idea of loving or accepting themselves. Because of their theological background they constantly see themselves as only insignificant worms to be stepped on, worthless sinners deserving only hell. They have a hard time blending the idea of a good self-image with what they know of the Bible. Quoting Romans 12:3, 'Do not think of yourself more highly than you ought, but rather think of yourself with sober judgment, in accordance with the measure of faith God has given you,' they say, 'You see, you *shouldn't* think highly of yourself; you should put yourself down.'

Contemporary secular psychologists see inconsistencies in such theological thinking. A renowned psychologist, Rollo May, said:

> In the circles where self-contempt is preached, it is of course never explained why a person should be so ill-mannered and inconsiderate as to force his company on other people if he finds it so dreary and deadening himself. And, furthermore, the multitude of contradictions are never adequately explained in a doctrine which advises that we should hate the one self, "I," and love all others, with the obvious expectation that they will love us, hateful creatures that we are; or that the more we hate ourselves, the more we love God who made the mistake, in an off moment, of creating this contemptible creature, "I". [8]

In Romans 12:3 Paul did not say that we should not think highly of ourselves. He said we should not think more highly of ourselves than *what we really are*. In other words, we should be realistic and biblical in our opinions of ourselves. That's why Paul added that we are 'to think so as to have sound judgment...' (NASB).

The verb *think* in the Greek means 'to think or feel a certain way about a person.'[9] In Romans 12:3 it means to form an opinion, a judgement, or a feeling about yourself. Paul's point is to form this opinion or self-concept as a result of a realistic appraisal of ourselves.

Paul's purpose in this passage was *not* to encourage people to avoid having a positive self-image. Rather, we are to develop a healthy self-image, or self-evaluation, that coincides with what God says about us. Granted, part of Paul's emphasis was to caution believers against pride or a haughty spirit. But the reverse of that emphasis cautions against false humility or self-deprecation. Here we see that Paul recognized the importance of having an appropriate self-image, one that incorporated an honest and realistic evaluation of one's God-given gifts and talents. The challenge of course is then to use these for the good of the entire body of Christ.

It's obvious that people are tremendously diverse in talents, spiritual gifts and abilities. Paul's deep concern was for unity in the body of Christ. The key to bringing unity in the midst of such diversity is for Christians to be honest in evaluating themselves and the gifts God has given then *for His service*. They should do that, however, without comparing themselves with others in attempts to see if they are superior or inferior. Paul said that those who compare themselves with others 'are without understanding.'[10] He also emphasized that we should not evaluate our gifts and abilities in order to exalt ourselves over others or to boast about our special characteristics. Rather we should look at ourselves and our God-given abilities as a basis from which to serve others.

Am I important to Christ?

The feeling of being important to Christ and to each other was intended to be the normal experience of our lives. It's a wonderful experience to be able to appraise yourself honestly and still feel good about who you are.

Christians who believe we should negate self and put ourselves down fail to stress that humankind also has great worth to God. This worth is not from what we have made of ourselves, however, but from what God has done for us and in us. We are fallen sinners, yet we still were created in God's image. We were, in fact, the crown of His creation— which gives all humankind intrinsic worth.

The Scriptures indicate that human beings are special to God in a number of ways. They are the apex of God's creation (Gen 1), created in the image of God (Gen 1:26–27), with each of us having the potential of becoming a child of God (Jn 1:12–13). You might say, as Francis Schaeffer has said, 'Man is sinful and wonderful.' In the Old Testament the Psalmist marvelled that we were created 'a little lower than the angels'[11] and are given a special purpose by God (Gen 1:28). The New Testament writers, too, acknowledge that human beings are a creation special to God. We are the objects of God's redemptive purposes in this world (Jn 3:16). As redeemed people, we even have angels watching over us (Heb 1:14; Ps 91:11–12; Dan 6:22; compare Mt 4:11) and Jesus Himself preparing a place for us in eternity (Jn 14:1–3).

Clearly, humankind has worth to God, individually and as a race.

Self-worth is not an idea foreign to Scripture. It is inter-woven into the heart of God's redemptive process. The One who bought us with a price knows our true worth. The price He paid for you and me is *Jesus* (1 Cor 6:20; 1 Pet 1:18–19). If you ever had to put a price tag on yourself, it would have to read 'Jesus'. His death on the cross was the payment for our sins. You are 'worth Jesus' to God because that is what He paid for you. That is His statement of your value. And God's view of you and your worth is the true one.

It's important, however, for us to realize that we have this intrinsic worth because of what God has done and who He made us to be. It is not a worth acquired by us—something *we* did or did not do to deserve it. In Ephesians 1:18 (LB), Paul wrote about our intrinsic worth: 'I want you to realize that God has been made rich because we who are Christ's have been given to him.'

So we see that the Scriptures validate the concept of self-worth without repudiating human sinfulness. For thousands of years philosophers and theologians have wrestled with these two aspects of our nature. On the one hand, human beings created in God's image have great value and are capable of kind, benevolent, loving behaviour. On the other hand, human beings are fallen, sinful, and have been responsible for history's cruelest events. We have produced Neros and Hitlers. Humanity's dignity and value, contrasted with its sinfulness, self-centredness and pride, are history's great contradiction.

But God's grace is shown in that, even though people are sinners in their fallen state, God considers them valuable enough to be 'purchased back', even when the price is something truly precious, the blood of Jesus (see Luke 15). This is the one and only solution for the paradox of human nature, a paradox for which secular psychologists have found no explanation. Only through a loving God's intervention can humankind's two natures be reconciled. That reconciliation is a divine solution, foreign to human intellect and understanding.

Isn't self-worth the same as pride?

The distinction between self-worth and pride is hard for some Christians to perceive, but the concepts are significantly different. *Self-worth* is a conviction that you have fundamental value because you were created by God in His image and because Jesus died for your sins.

Pride points to self. It is rooted in the pleasure you find in yourself for what you believe you can do or have done with your life. Pride is an attitude of superiority, a puffed-up mentality, that manifests itself in an arrogant, unrealistic estimation of oneself in relation to others (1 Cor 4:6–7, 18–19; 5:2; 8:1–2; 13:4). Admonitions can be found throughout Scripture about God's opposition to pride and a haughty spirit: 'God opposes the proud, but gives grace to the humble.'[12] 'Pride goes before destruction.'[13]

Sometimes Christians fall into the trap of wanting people to glorify or praise them, not God, because of what He has done in their lives. Such thinking is a perversion of Galatians 1:24, 'And they gave glory to God because of me' (LB), and a distortion of the response of the Psalmist, 'I will give *thanks to Thee,* for I am fearfully and wonderfully made' (Ps 139:14, NASB).

This book is not an effort to promote pride or false

humility but to encourage appreciation, thankfulness and joy for all that Christ has done in each of us.

Our success comes through Christ

A lot of Christians today are emphasizing the importance of being a success, a winner. That, too, can lead to pride when the emphasis is on the goal or end result and not on the source of success, Jesus Christ. To teach that Christians should be winners, some use verses like 'God...gives us the victory through our Lord Jesus Christ'[14] and 'In all these things we win an overwhelming victory through him who has proved his love for us.'[15] Sometimes, however, the emphasis is put on being a winner and not on the idea common to both verses, 'through Christ', which is the basis for being a success. Without an emphasis on the phrase 'through Christ', the teaching that Christians should be winners can foster pride. With this phrase, it can foster a healthy self-image and walk of faith to the glory of God.

Pride is the result of an exaltation of oneself out of failure to recognize who made us who we are. Elizabeth Skoglund writes:

> Many people confuse the distinctions among pride, humility, and good self-esteem. The problem is not that *self-esteem* contradicts the Scriptures but rather that the words pride and humility are not correctly understood in the total light of Scripture. *Pride* in the biblical sense involves a not-honest estimate of oneself. Real *humility* is simply an absence of concentration upon oneself. It means that while I like and accept myself I don't need to prove my worth excessively either to myself or to others (italics added).[16]

I would go even further in defining humility as 'knowing who you are, knowing who made you who you are, and giving God the glory for it.' Somehow we associate humility with an attitude of self-deprecation. 'I'm nothing; I can't do anything; I'm a failure; I'm a sinner; God can't use me; oh, how rotten I am' and on and on and on. True humility not only recognizes one's own sinfulness, one's shortcomings or feelings of 'rottenness', but also acknowledges the image of God that is in us, one's God-given abilities, talents and individual personality. In humility we acknowledge our weaknesses and strengths, our shortcomings and abilities, our limitations and specialness, all in the light of who we are in Christ. So humility includes not only being grateful for your abilities but also trusting God for your inadequacies.

I saw a clear example of humility at the Amsterdam 83 Itinerant Evangelists Conference, attended by four thousand evangelists from all over the world, most of them from third world countries. During the question-and-answer session with Billy Graham, a man from Africa yelled out, 'Billy, if you were not white and an American, where would you be today?' One can well understand the implications of that question. The crowd fell quiet, awaiting Graham's answer. Without hesitation Billy lovingly and emphatically responded, 'I am who I am by the grace of God.'

For a moment there was silence and then a great round of applause. Billy Graham knows who he is, who made him who he is, and he gives God the glory for it. A healthy self-image acknowledges the workmanship of Christ that is innate in our being.

Humility is often the channel for God's glory. Our Creator can be glorified not only through our abilities but also through our weaknesses. That is the thrust of my biography, *A Sceptic's Quest*, written by Joe Musser. Joe points out that many of my areas of weakness and limitation have become my greatest areas of strength and of glorifying God. We all have limitations and weaknesses. What counts is how we deal with them. Are we repelled by them or do we accept them realistically and then try to change or improve these areas?

A healthy sense of self-worth is fundamental in drawing us closer to God; it elevates our concept of God who gave us such worth. A sense of pride, however, leads us to self-worship and to usurping God's right to control our life. A healthy self-image also elevates in our mind the worth of others, whom we are to consider 'more highly than ourselves'.

Without a healthy self-image we become preoccupied with ourselves, concentrating on our own needs. We constantly 'position ourselves' in order to be accepted by others.

Once we see ourselves as God sees us, and realize who we are—that we're uniquely made in God's image and are loved, accepted, forgiven—we are set free from self-preoccupation, to being concerned for other people.

Servanthood seems to have its roots in a healthy self-image. If you feel threatened by others because of a poor self-image, then you usually try to overcome that threat by making others look bad or by struggling to make yourself look better. You are likely to feel threatened by the role of serving others, when it means treating someone else as more important than yourself. Some Christian people with poor self-images assume that serving will cause God and others to think better of them. A Christian with a healthy self-image, however, will eagerly enter the role of being a servant to others with 'no strings attached'.

What kind of self-love is OK?

A premise with both scriptural and psychological validity is that you can love others only after accepting yourself. The phrase 'Love your neighbour as yourself' is stated five times in the Bible (Lev 19:18; Mt 19:19; Mk 12:31; Lk 10:27; Rom 13:9). It is listed by Jesus as the second greatest commandment. Today it is often used by Christian writers and speakers to support the concept of self-worth or self-love.

We must first take note, however, that we are not commanded to love ourselves in these passages. Self-love is assumed. Jesus and the authors of Scripture imply that self-love is a normal experience. They assume that the people to whom they are speaking or writing already love themselves.

> *Having a healthy self-esteem*
> *is not our ultimate goal.*
> *Knowing Christ in all His*
> *fullness is.*

Paul made a similar assumption in his letter to the Ephesians. 'Husbands ought to love their wives as their own bodies. He who loves his wife loves himself. After all, no-one ever hated his own body.'[17] Because the Scriptures assume a normal, natural self-love, rather than telling us to hate ourselves, we can conclude that to have a feeling of self-love or self-concern is biblical. The Bible assumes that we are already concerned about our own well-being.

It is important to realize that we should not make the development of a healthy self-esteem our supreme priority. In reality, a positive self-image is a by-product of pursuing the goal of knowing Christ and of being conformed to His image. Having a healthy self-esteem is not our ultimate goal. Knowing Christ in all His fullness is.

Building a better self-image

Rewrite your strong points listed at the end of chapter one. Then, considering each strong point individually, determine whether or not you have used it as a basis for erroneous pride ('Look at what I have or what I have done') or of valid self-worth ('God has graciously given me this characteristic, which confirms the value He sees in me').

Strong Points	Pride	Self-Worth
_____	_____	_____
_____	_____	_____
_____	_____	_____
_____	_____	_____
_____	_____	_____

Rewrite the weaknesses you listed at the end of chapter one. Then consider these areas of weakness and decide if you've used them as a basis of self-deprecation or false humility, or if you have yielded each one to Christ (2 Cor 12:9).

Weak Points	Self-deprecation	Yielded to Christ
_____	_____	_____
_____	_____	_____
_____	_____	_____
_____	_____	_____
_____	_____	_____

3

Results of a Poor Self-Image

One of the most profound effects of a poor self-image can be seen in the attitude a person develops towards his or her world. Persons with an unhealthy self-image have a fearful, pessimistic view of the world and of their ability to cope with its challenges. They see unexpected or new situations as threats to their personal happiness and security, seemingly planned as attacks on them personally. They see the world as closing in on them, pushing and crushing them.

Joanna, an attractive woman, said, 'A worm doesn't adequately describe how I feel about myself. A worm can crawl underground and hide; he doesn't leave a trail behind him. I'm more like the ugly, slimy slugs on my patio. Everywhere they go they leave this horrible trail behind them. I'm like them; I mess up everything wherever I go.'

World

Such people tend to receive what the world sends their way without challenging or attempting to change it. They see themselves as victims, helplessly entrapped in a hostile environment.

On the other hand, persons with a healthy self-esteem see the world as a challenge to be faced, an opportunity to exercise personal strength and trust in Christ. Such people assume they can have an impact on their world through Christ, and that by the grace of God they can effectively change their environment. They believe their destiny lies in what Christ can do through them, that they can and should accomplish significant things for eternity with their lives.

World

A poor self-image affects different people in different ways, but some similarities exist from person to person. For some people the effects are conscious; for others the effects are unconscious, deceiving them secretly.

We see the world through our self-image

Our perceptions and interpretations of the world around us are affected by the picture we have of ourselves. A poor self-image distorts the messages we receive from people and the way we interpret the events in life. That is why a poor self-image is hard to correct. It filters out any positive messages, whether from God or others. Those positive messages are needed if we are to change the opinion we have of ourselves.

Anyone who does much counselling is aware of the discounting or rejection of praise that many habitually practise whenever someone offers them a compliment. All of us know people who have trouble accepting praise. Not receiving or hearing positive things about ourselves is a similar process, one that keeps us from changing. Somewhere inside, we already have made a decision about our worth. Until that decision is changed, we will be unable to alter our self-image.

Persons with weak self-images don't like themselves. They even have trouble expressing how badly they feel about themselves. Like Joanna, the feelings these people have about themselves might be termed *self-disgust*.

Persons with a weak or unhealthy self-image operate in life from any number of these perceived factors and motivations:

1. Pessimistic outlook on life
2. Lack of confidence in social skills
3. Extreme sensitivity to the opinions of other people
4. Self-consciousness about appearance, performance or status
5. A view of other people as competition to beat, not friends to enjoy
6. A sense of masculinity or femininity felt only through sexual conquests
7. A striving to become something or somebody instead of relaxing and enjoying who they are
8. A view of the present as something to be pushed aside, focusing instead on past achievements or future dreams
9. Fear of God or belief that He is uninterested or angry with them
10. A habit of mentally going over past conversations or situations, wondering what the other person meant
11. A critical and judgemental view of others

12. Defensiveness in behaviour and conversations
13. An attitude of carrying a chip on their shoulder
14. Use of anger as a defence to keep from getting hurt
15. A tendency to develop clinging relationships
16. Inability to accept praise
17. Self-defeating habits and patterns of behaviour
18. A habit of letting others 'walk' on them
19. Fear of being alone
20. Fear of intimacy, because it might lead to rejection or a smothering relationship
21. A problem in believing or accepting God's love or the love of another person
22. Dependence on material possessions for security
23. Inability to express emotions
24. A habit of using negative labels in referring to themselves
25. Anticipation or worry that the worst will happen
26. A tendency to follow the crowd and avoid independent behaviour
27. Perfectionistic behaviour regarding details
28. Perpetually rigid, legalistic and ritualistic preferences in worship
29. Interpretation of their world as hostile and over-powering
30. A shifting of responsibility to others for unwanted or negative situations or feelings
31. Need for lots of structure and external control in life
32. Overly sensitive conscience

First, a word of caution. At this point, be careful not to overreact to the above list. A poor self-image is not the sole cause of all those factors. There may be many other causes. For example, many of the above tendencies can be caused also by outright unconfessed sin or rebellion. Further, just because someone has extremely poor self-esteem doesn't mean that all these factors will be true of their lives.

People with a poor self-image often practise what may be called 'the double put-down'. They either put themselves down, hoping someone else will disagree with them and build them up, or they put down someone else in order to build themselves up.

Without self-acceptance it is hard to love or accept someone else. If you don't have a healthy self-acceptance, you'll continually try to prove yourself to yourself and to other people. Your lifestyle will be one of trying to *get* instead of trying to *give*.

If you don't have a good self-image, it is difficult to accept yourself the way you are. And you usually can't trust someone else to accept you the way you are. You begin to project a person who isn't really you. When a person gets married on that basis, trouble comes fast, even in Christian marriages.

Self-image affects marriage

A poor self-image is one of the prime causes of problems in marital intimacy today. If you don't have a healthy self-acceptance, how can you expect your mate to accept you for who you are? You can't, and so you start to build a façade or barrier around yourself. As a result, the man or woman who marries you gets married to a façade, not to a real person. When that happens, the façade gets larger and larger and, usually, any intimacy that was in the initial relationship disappears. Persons who don't have good self-acceptance focus on getting their own needs met (often accomplishing that badly) and not on meeting the needs of their mate. This fits right in with what Rollo May said about Christians continuing to look down on themselves, thinking they are being spiritual by doing so.

Even in the famous American Masters and Johnson sex-therapy clinics, less than ten per cent of the time with clients is spent dealing with the physical aspects of sex.

Ninety per cent of the time is spent dealing with self-esteem and communication. So often the sources of sexual problems are in those areas and not in the physical aspect itself.

Today's lack of absolutes together with our poor self-images have resulted in our using sex to try to build up our self-esteem. That results, instead, in demeaning both self and the other person.

So much of what we see in sexual practice these days are people trying to prove themselves. You've got to prove you're a man and can satisfy a woman. You've got to prove you're a woman and can please a man and yourself sexually.

A lot of that frenzied pressure comes from a sense of 'I don't like myself and I've got to prove my worth.' When you see yourself as God sees you, know who you are and really like yourself—acknowledging your weaknesses and your strong points—when you are obedient by faith, you're not so influenced by peer pressure. If you're single and you have a good self-image, you don't have to use a boyfriend or girlfriend to buoy up your self-esteem. If you're married, you don't have to use your mate to build yourself up. You don't have to prove yourself to yourself or to anyone else in order to accept yourself. You are satisfied with God's evaluation of who you are.

Building a better self-image

3

Read Psalm 139:13–16 (preferably in the Living Bible). Write in your own words what these verses tell you about yourself.

_____

_____

_____

Can you honestly thank God for making you the way He did?

(Answer yes or no.) _____ If not, can you thank Him by faith, asking Him also to show you how you can be thankful for the way He made you? (Answer yes or no.)

_____

Write out a prayer expressing thanks to God, to the degree that you are able, for making you who you are.

_____

_____

_____

_____

_____

_____

4

How You Decided Who You Are

From early childhood on, we assimilate information both from authority figures and from peers so we can evaluate ourselves in three important areas of life: appearance, performance, importance. Their combined responses form a major portion of what we think ourselves to be—our self-image.

Responses from others are important to us not only in childhood but in adulthood as well. After we've grown up, we still gather data to confirm who and what we think we are—perhaps from different sources. Although the initial evaluation of ourselves is completed early in life and is difficult to change, we keep on seeking input from peers and friends so that we can know what kinds of persons we are today.

How do I look?

James Dobson in *Hide or Seek,* (Revell, 1974) says that the most highly valued personal attribute in our culture is physical attractiveness. The first question we seek to answer is 'How do I look?' We formulate a mental image of ourselves from the praise or ridicule of other people. We evaluate ourselves by their reactions to our physical appearance.

The importance of this area to our self-esteem is illustrated by the millions of pounds we spend each year on clothes, cosmetics and beauty aids, and by the amount of time we spend just arranging and checking our dress and personal appearance. Further millions are spent on cosmetic surgery. People today have everything 'fixed' from their noses to their navels. If our physical appearance is 'picture perfect', we think we can feel good about ourselves.

The importance of physical attractiveness can be illustrated by the difficulties of Susan, a young career woman, whose job required her to be with other attractive young women daily. Her personal sense of physical inadequacy, however, affected her ability to relax in her work.

Since her teenage years, Susan's mother had told her that she wasn't shaped right. Yet judged by contemporary standards, she was attractive. Nonetheless she felt ugly and inadequate in comparison with the women with whom she worked. She was convinced that no man would ever like her because her figure wasn't 'perfect'. Her insecurity about herself so interfered with her work that eventually she lost her job.

Sam suffered from a severe disfigurement, the result of a childhood accident. An explosion had torn his lips when he was just a toddler. Over the years numerous attempts at cosmetic surgery had been unsuccessful. As a teenager he suffered rejection from his peers, particularly from girls. He retreated to a life of withdrawal and loneliness. At one point he was spending ten to twenty hours a week escaping to the unreal world of films. In his struggle to be accepted, his disfigurement and the resulting rejection also caused him to be overly compliant.

You and I, too, are influenced in the feelings we have about ourselves by the way we think we look. What we see in the mirror is interpreted largely by others' opinions about us that we hear and remember. (Some people may have had different opinions about us, but we either don't hear them or choose not to hear them.) That is particularly true during our school years.

Bob's parents may have told him that he was the most handsome boy in town, but when he got to school the children there pointed out whatever faults they thought he had. There have always been children who have come home from school in tears because they were teased about being fat or having red hair, freckles, curly hair or goofy teeth. Such memories live on within us even as adults.

That need for a 'perfect' outward appearance extends beyond our immediate physical appearance. How many times do people think, 'Oh, if I could only have this car or that friend, then I would be accepted. Then I, too, could think better of myself.'

How am I doing?

A second big question we ask ourselves, 'How am I doing?' refers to our performance. A companion question is, 'How am I doing in comparison with others?' We live in a performance-work-oriented society. We tend therefore to formulate a mental image of ourselves that is based on our successes or failures in the eyes of our parents and peers.

If our image of our competence is shallow, we will feel threatened when someone else succeeds. Or, when we hear of someone else's weaknesses or failures, a sense of pride may build up within us.

Glad you couldn't come. I've known these feelings from personal experience. One of the top Christian speakers in the USA is Dick Purnell, a dear friend (he was my room-mate during our Wheaton College days). I suggested him as an alternative speaker for a large singles' conference in Florida, since I wasn't able to attend. 'But we don't know Dick,' the conference leader said. 'Just take my word for it,' I replied. 'They'll love him.'

After the conference the director phoned me and

jokingly, without realizing the connotation of his words, said, 'Boy, are we glad you couldn't come!' For a few minutes there, Dick loomed as a very big threat to me— before I sorted through my feelings. Later, however, I was able to share the story with others and say, 'You know, that was one of the most special things I've heard this year.'

A few months passed, and again I was asked to speak at a singles' seminar in Chicago, this one for airline personnel. Again I couldn't go, so I recommended Dick. Afterwards, I met a flight attendant on a plane who had been at the conference. 'Oh,' she said, 'it was great that you were ill! Everyone just loved Dick!' And, do you know, this time thankfulness for Dick and his abilities as a communicator welled up in me immediately.

When I got home I told my wife, 'After twice lining up Dick to speak in my place and then finding people over-joyed that I couldn't make it, I really am glad my self-image is good.' Not too many years ago such responses would have threatened me and my friendship with Dick. Now I wish there were a hundred Dick Purnells to send in my place.

The work addiction. An example of a person who is seek-ing to build up his or her self-image through performance is the *workaholic.* Many of us have a touch of this trait in our personalities. Ministers and Christian workers are often plagued with the problem. We feel good about ourselves when we are very busy, when we have accomplished many things, when we are dog-tired from working long, long hours. Our self-image is closely tied to our performance. One woman said, 'I really feel good at night when I'm so tired I can hardly move.'

A friend of mine tells me that this is a pattern of behaviour familiar to him, one he has always fought. He was raised in a loving home, yet no matter how well he performed a given task, his parents always wanted him to do better. He was never told that he had done a good job.

His parents' approval, particularly his father's, always seemed to be just out of reach. He felt like the proverbial donkey reaching for the carrot dangling before his nose— or like a greyhound at the dog races, chasing a rabbit that can never be caught. He expressed his frustration metaphorically when he said, 'I'm always climbing the ladder, but never reaching the top.'

Today he still finds himself working to hear words of approval from his parents. Both of them are dead, but their standards still live on within him. He still struggles against the drive to try to reach those parental standards.

If you want to test your own workaholic tendencies, pay attention to how easy it is for you to relax. Can you take a day or so and do nothing? Can you sit still for a long period of time, and not work or read, without anxiety rising? Workaholics often get depressed when their achievement level is hindered either by choice (holidays, days off, weekends), or by circumstances (illness, old age, loss of job). People with workaholic tendencies need to do something all the time in order to feel good about themselves, to have a sense of self-acceptance.

> *All of us have formulated a mental image of ourselves based on the feelings of acceptance we received from our parents.*

How important am I?

A third question used to define who we are, is 'How important am I?' It deals with our status. It's related to our ability to control or influence our group, the sense of power we have within our own group. So many people feel that if they can get in a position of power in politics or in business, then they'll feel better about themselves and be better accepted. How ironic it is that many business people who are marvellously successful still think of themselves as failures.

All of us have formulated a mental image of ourselves based on the feelings of acceptance we received from our parents. As children we were concerned with how much our parents liked us and how important we were to them. W. Hugh Missildine has a number of statements relevant to this point in his book, *Your Inner Child of the Past:*

> A child develops his sense of being as a worthwhile, capable, important, and unique individual from the attention given him by his parents. He "sees" or feels himself reflected in their love, approval, and attention to his needs....
>
> In childhood, in order to win the warmth, affection, and attention of his parents, the child absorbs and imitates even the gestures and grimaces of his parents as well as their way of looking at himself and the world in general. The most important of these attitudes is...how the parent feels about the child. This determines how the child feels about himself. He has no other guide, no other mirror that reflects what kind of a person he is and whether he is worth loving.[1]

One of the ways we worked out how important we were to our parents was by the amount of time they spent with us. We learnt early in life that more important things take up more time than less important things. A child who is always forced to take second place to a job, television or the newspaper comes to feel unloved.

The daughter of a friend of mine was three years old when this issue was brought into much sharper focus for him and his wife. They had just moved into a new house and were up to their elbows in landscaping. Having set out twenty young azalea bushes (plants that take a lot of special care), his wife was spending lots of time daily caring for these and other plants. One morning their daughter was watching her mother work on the azaleas, diligently pouring her soul into each one. From the depths of the three-year-old's inner being came the disturbing question, 'Mum, do you love me as much as you do your flowers?'

As children we develop an understanding of the 'priority of importance'. Important people and things get first priority and receive lots of time and attention. We rate ourselves by the amount of time and attention we receive.

As adults we still rate ourselves

Though we are no longer children, we still use people's attitudes and reactions towards us to answer those three questions: How do I look? How am I doing? How important am I?

When we perceive that people react positively towards us, we feel good about ourselves. When their attitudes and reactions are negative, we feel bad. Further, as mentioned before, a poor self-image from childhood will continue to cause us to filter out the positive attitudes and reactions and to concentrate only on the negative.

We're like a circus elephant tied down by a bicycle chain. We ask how one small chain could hold a powerful elephant. The trainer explains that the chain doesn't hold him; it's the elephant's memory that keeps him from trying to escape.

When the elephant was very young, he didn't have the strength to break the chain or pull free. He learnt then that the chain was stronger than he was and he hasn't forgotten that. The result is that the elephant, now full-grown and powerful, remembers only that he tried to break the chain and couldn't. So he never tries again. His memory, not the chain, binds him. Of course, occasionally an elephant does discover he can break the chain, and from then on his keeper has trouble controlling him.

Our self-image works in a similar manner. We learn about our strengths and weaknesses as children and those memories keep us bound as an adult. The experiences we had—the good ones and the painful ones—are imprinted on our subconscious mind and we go through life still believing we are the same person with the same weaknesses we thought were ours so many years ago. The childhood feelings we remember are fully alive today and remind us that the world around us was, and assumedly still is, stronger than we are.

But like a breakaway elephant, we can experience freedom from those bonds within us. No longer need those feelings of acceptance or rejection keep us oblivious to the God-given qualities and strengths that now are ours.

Building a better self-image

4

Ephesians 1:11 in the Living Bible states, 'Because of what Christ has done we have become *gifts* to God that he *delights* in.'

What does the word *delight* mean? _____

_____

Who have become 'gifts'? _____

To whom were these gifts given? _____

What does He do with these gifts? _____

Does that mean that God delights in you? _____

Hebrews 12:2 reads, 'Let us fix our eyes on Jesus, the author and perfecter of our faith, who for the *joy* set before him endured the cross.'

Whom does the 'joy' refer to in this verse? _____

5

Growing Up With Mum and Dad

Have you ever considered God's plan for developing a person? The production of a healthy personality and adequate self-image doesn't happen by accident. By specific design, God planned for two persons, one male and one female, to produce an offspring. The need for male and female parents has to do with biological procreation, but it also has to do with the process of growing healthy personalities and individuals who have adequate self-images.

God planned the growth process that requires human offspring to spend many years in various stages of dependency. It's a process that includes physical, spiritual and emotional development. He established the parenting process as its corollary. Both processes are fundamental in His plan for growing a healthy person.

The importance of these two processes can be understood when we stop to consider the amount of time spent in each. The physical growth process usually takes eighteen years. The parenting process involves approximately the same. This means that the average person will spend at least half of life as a part of the parenting process, either in being parented or in parenting.

For example, the Reeses were involved in the growth and parenting processes for thirty-six years. There was an eighteen-year span between the oldest and youngest of their four children. Add to that the eighteen years they were parented themselves and you have more than half a century of being involved in growth and parenting. And that calculation doesn't include the many years the Reeses served as delightful grandparents to their thirteen grand-children.

Since God designed the growth and parenting processes to require such a large portion of the brief years of our lives, they must be important to Him. From the beginning He established those two processes as foundational in pro-ducing healthy personalities and adequate self-concepts. One of the greatest activities human beings can give their lives to is fulfilling God's first commandment, to be fruitful and multiply.

Parents are God's agents

As has been said, the initial development of our self-image lies in our relationships with our parents. Self-images are most of all derived from the authority figures to whom we were in submission in childhood. We learnt who we were and what we were like from them. 'A child literally discovers what kind of a person he is and how he feels about himself by the reactions of his parents to him.'[1]

Our parents' evaluations of us were transferred to our young minds. We saw ourselves in the light of their thoughts and actions towards us. From their attitudes we sensed their feelings about us. Those experiences, even if long ago forgotten, served to form our self-concepts.

Thus the everyday experiences of our childhood (not solely the traumatic ones) were what shaped our self-images. The general atmosphere in our families contributed more to our view of ourselves than any single event. We adopted the general attitude of our families, internalizing those feelings. Understanding that influence is a significant ingre-dient in our attempts to see our self-image transformed.

A well-known counsellor and writer, Cecil Osborne, says, 'The young child has no clear picture of himself. He sees himself only in the mirror of his parents' evaluation of himself.... A child who is told repeatedly that he is a bad boy, or is lazy, or no good or stupid or shy or clumsy, will tend to act out this picture which the parent or some other authority figure has given him.'[2]

Larry, for example, had a deep-seated depression and lack of confidence in himself. At twenty-six, he still hadn't found what he wanted to do with his life. He was frustrated, insecure, and felt very inadequate. His father had always called him 'stupid' (even today his father still tells him that and says he can't do anything). Larry's self-image is distorted. He feels that he is what his father always said he was.

Is there a recipe for a good family?

The psychologist Stanley Coopersmith in *The Antecedents of Self-Esteem* describes some of the characteristics of a family that builds self-esteem in its children. The most significant characteristic is an attitude of unconditional acceptance and love. This attitude is a *constant*; it is not something given or withdrawn depending on a child's behaviour.[3]

The second characteristic is an attitude of understanding. Children think that their parents know and really grasp how they feel. If children are not allowed to express their feelings, positive and negative, then they don't know that they are understood. They feel unacceptable because their feelings are unacceptable.

It's interesting to note in Coopersmith's study that children with a good sense of self-worth were disciplined as often as children of the same age who lacked self-confidence. The differences in the results of discipline appear to be related to the parents' focus during the disciplining process.

Children who communicated a better sense of self-worth were those who had been disciplined for displaying offensive or inappropriate behaviour. Those who had a lower sense of self-worth had been disciplined for being 'bad children'. It's important to distinguish between a child's behaviour, which may be offensive, and the child himself or herself, who is loved.

> *If parents knew how important they are in their children's development, perhaps they would work harder to have an affirming attitude in their relationships with their children.*

If parents knew how important they are in their children's development, perhaps they would work harder to have an affirming attitude in their relationships with their children. Regrettably, often that isn't the case. Our parents, many of whom suffered from poor self-images themselves, find it difficult to give to us what they didn't have. In their own sense of inadequacy it was easy for them to communicate negative feelings to us when we were children.

Peers also play a role

A second influence on our self-concept is the input we receive from friends, classmates and teachers. Our peers help shape our self-images too. They either confirm or deny what we have been taught at home.

Think of the little girl who was told at home how nice and pretty she was. One day she entered school and was crushed because someone called her 'carrot-top' or 'freckles'. Or consider the young boy who believed he was a good athlete until he got to school where he found he was clumsy and couldn't do many of the things the other children could do.

Children can be cruel. Their name-calling and jokes hurt. They cut deep and chop away at the positive aspects of our self-images. The more sensitive we are as children, the deeper are the wounds made by our classmates' humour and harassment.

On the other hand, a seminary professor told how this process worked positively in his case. He had been raised in an unhappy home; his mother had deserted the family when he was quite young. His father was in the army, so the boy spent most of his time with grandparents.

His first few years of school were miserable. Branded early on as a problem child, he lived up to that label. Then one year when entering a new class, he was greeted at the door by a very wise teacher. She looked him straight in the eye, called him by name and said, 'I've heard all about you, but I don't believe a word of it!' That day was the turning point in his young life, the professor now says. Someone believed in him! Substitute parents or authority figures, usually teachers or close relatives, can sometimes be life-savers for parentally deprived children.

Another dominant influence on the self-images of children are brothers and sisters, although theirs is not usually so strong an influence as parents or peers outside the home. In some cases, however, an only child suddenly and unpreparedly 'de-throned' by a new baby in the house has a marked change in self-image. Sometimes two children of the same sex who are close in age can strongly affect one another's self-image. An older child who has to take on a parenting role of younger children also can have an altered self-concept.

God has ideals for parents

The ideal parenting process that God set up was for every child to have a positive and close relationship with two parents—that is, input and influence from both a male and a female parent. The healthy development of the human personality requires this interaction with masculine and feminine authority figures during the eighteen years of childhood and adolescence.

This is God's design for human children. No offspring in the animal world appears to have this requirement or need because no other created being has a personality like the human being. Two parents are necessary for procreation; they are also necessary to reveal the character of God to children. Together, in their 'one flesh' relationship, the parents communicate and demonstrate God's attributes to their children. Through this interaction the children have all the necessary ingredients to become healthy persons who can entrust their lives to God, their heavenly Parent.

Sometimes, however, parents sacrifice long-range goals (of Christian character for their children) on the altar of immediate objectives. They choose to have quiet, well-behaved children; the children are frightened into obedience so that the parents' friends comment on how well-behaved they are. Parents can be so rigid that the children dare not step out of line, and that is unhealthy.

In child rearing, the means determines the end. With the right means any child can be coerced, for a time, into behaviour a parent might desire. Parental success, however, is not measured when the child is six or sixteen, but when the child is thirty-six. Parents have to live with the fruit of their labours for many years. The true results of these labours are seen only in their adult offspring.

God structured human personality development to be a long process. He chose to have even His human Son born of a female parent. Jesus was parented through infancy and childhood very much like other children of His day. The parenting process was not set aside for Him; it was used to help Him grow to manhood.

From the Scriptures we can determine three important ingredients of the parenting process. Although the Bible doesn't give us detailed instructions on how to be a parent, it does provide an outline of God's strategy.

The first ingredient is *modelling*. Parents serve as models for their children, whether or not they are aware of it. The question is, What kind of models will they be? Children observe and imitate parents' words, behaviour and attitudes. They learn to think what their parents think, feel what they feel, choose what they choose and behave in a manner similar to their parents.

The second ingredient in the parenting process is *teaching*. Parents are to teach their children procedures and principles for living. It includes everything from learning how to tie a shoe to the scriptural truth of who God is. Biblically, teaching includes not only verbal instruction but, when necessary, discipline to enforce the teaching.

The third ingredient is *learning to relate*. Parents are to love their children and relate to them in a tender, caring way. All three of these ingredients are important in the parenting process, but learning to relate is most crucial. Without a warm, loving, emotionally intimate relationship, the other two ingredients will be ineffective in the child's life.

The Bible pictures three healthy personalities

If parents could fulfil God's original strategy today, they would produce children with healthy personalities who could come to entrust their lives to their heavenly Father. In the Scriptures three healthy personalities provide examples of what God intended us to be. The first two are Adam and Eve before the Fall. By observing these two perfect creations of a perfect God, we can see some of what it means to be mentally healthy. The third truly healthy personality is Jesus Christ. His personality was untouched by sin, so in Him there is a perfect picture of a truly healthy person.

The New Testament presents Jesus Christ as a model of our Christian growth. Time and time again the writers hold Him up as the One we are to be like. Each person who accepts Christ eventually is to become like Him.

> ... for whom I am again in the pains of childbirth until Christ is formed in you.[4]

> ... until we all reach unity in the faith and in the knowledge of the Son of God and become mature, attaining to the whole measure of the fulness of Christ.[5]

> Instead, speaking the truth in love, we will in all things grow up into him who is the Head, that is, Christ.[6]

> ... to present you holy in his sight, without blemish and free from accusation.[7]

> ... so that we may present everyone perfect in Christ.[8]

Christians are to live a life that manifests Christ's characteristics to the world. They are not just to act like Christ but to become like Him in all of their personality. Paul clarified what it means to be like Christ in three New Testament passages. 'The fruit of the Spirit is love, joy, peace, patience, kindness, goodness, faithfulness, gentleness and self-control.'[9] The second passage, 1 Timothy 3, gives attributes that leaders of the church are to have. These are summarized in Titus 1:6–8:

> An elder must be blameless, the husband of but one wife, a man whose children believe and are not open to the charge of

being wild and disobedient. Since an overseer is entrusted with God's work, he must be blameless—not overbearing, not quick-tempered, not given to much wine, not violent, not pursuing dishonest gain. Rather he must be hospitable, one who loves what is good, who is self-controlled, upright, holy and disciplined.

Those three passages give a detailed picture of what a person who was truly like Christ would be like. Such a person would manifest the fruits of the Spirit and exhibit the characteristics and qualities of an elder. Those three lists also are the best picture available today of the attributes of a truly healthy personality.

Most Christians see 'becoming like Christ' as the goal towards which they are moving. Some Christians, however, add to their problems of self-esteem by comparing themselves as they are now with Christ, who is the highest model in the universe. Such persons often give up hope because they feel they can never meet His standard. They focus only on the goal and not on the process as well.

Christians need to keep a balanced perspective in the way they view themselves. They need to look forwards towards what they are to become—like Christ (which keeps us humble and sensitive to God's leading.) They also need to look backwards to what they were when they first accepted Christ (which makes us thankful and gives us hope). That kind of balance serves to keep Christians 'sober' in their view of themselves (Rom 12:3).

God's ideal became distorted

With the Fall of humankind, sin entered the world and God's ideal was destroyed. Because of sin there were no parents who could accurately manifest God's character and attributes to their children. Children grew up in an atmosphere and in relationships that gave them distorted pictures of God. When the children's own sinful natures reacted to those distorted pictures, the results were not healthy and whole personalities, but unhealthy, sinful persons who produced unhealthy, sinful personalities in their children. The Bible records the resulting cycle and its effect upon following generations in Exodus 20:5 and 34:7.

The parenting process was no longer what God wanted it to be, so children no longer had their emotional and spiritual needs met. Because of the sins of their parents, they had a faulty image of God and a distrust of Him. Modern society is the ongoing result of the cycle.

The scars that children pick up through the parenting process can be seen as vulnerabilities to certain kinds of sin. Every person has a 'sin nature' and will be involved in sin, but usually that is in the area of vulnerabilities acquired in childhood. Some adulterers would never think of hitting anyone. Others who have killed a person would never think of cheating on their mates.

When sin entered the world and parents failed to meet the God-given, innate needs of their children, the children began to look to the world to have those needs fulfilled. The parents didn't offer a healthy love, so the children sought love in sinful ways. Today, the process goes on, even in Christian homes.

We see stages of parental influence

Within God's ideal plan, the parental role in the development of children follows certain observable patterns. A child's development involves three stages of parental influence:

1. *The two-parent stage* (from birth to age three). Both parents are experienced by the child as nurturers during this stage.
2. *The opposite-sex parent stage* (age three to puberty). The parent of the opposite sex has the more significant

role in personality development.

3. *The same-sex parent stage* (puberty to adulthood). The parent of the same sex has the more significant impact on the child's development.

It is important for a child to have the influence of both parents during the entire developmental process, but it is also important that the child have the correct parental influence during these different stages. This is what makes the parenting process so difficult and challenging.

For a single parent, a child's grandparent can sometimes become the model for the missing parent, as happened in Billy's case. Billy's mum, who was divorced, worked for me. His father had disappeared and never saw Billy. Billy's mum eventually decided to move near her parents so her dad could become a positive male influence on Billy. That was ten years ago. Meeting Billy today you realize that her decision to move was a wise one.

The two-parent stage. Initially, during the first year to eighteen months of life, every child relates more to the female parent. In fact, researchers tell us that during these first eighteen months or so the child sees both parents as mothering figures. It's important during this period for the father to participate in the mothering role as much as possible.

At about three years of age, a child begins to discover that he is like Daddy or she is like Mother. This awareness of a distinct anatomical similarity to one parent marks the beginning of a change in the relationship to both parents.

The opposite-sex parent stage. From about age three to puberty, the parent of the opposite sex has the greater psychological significance on a child's development, although the same-sex parent plays a significant balancing role.

The child's interest in the opposite-sex parent is related to God's plan. God intended for the child's interest to be focused across sexual lines for development, as well as in programming for later relationships with the opposite sex. This stage of the opposite-sex parent's influence is the time when children are often referred to as 'Mummy's little boy' or 'Daddy's little girl.' It is the time when the child wants to possess that parent.

During this stage a child is prepared by the parent of the opposite sex to feel comfortable in adult relationships with the opposite sex. In this stage the child needs much nurturing, love, attention, and affection from the opposite-sex parent. Available research indicates that it is the warm, affectionate delight of the opposite-sex parent during these years that prepares a person for healthy, adult sexual relationships.

Time and time again it has been demonstrated that individuals who did not have adequate nurturing, love, attention, and affection during this stage from the opposite-sex parent have problems with sexual relationships as adults. A young girl who learned to feel comfortable in Daddy's arms will usually feel comfortable in her husband's arms. A young boy who knew his mother's delight will fully enjoy the delight of his wife.

Until about ten years of age, a child needs lots of touching, hugging, kissing, wrestling and snuggling from the parent of the opposite sex. During these years a child cannot receive too much healthy affection.

The same-sex parent stage. The third stage in a child's development, beginning at about puberty and lasting into adult years, is the time when the parent of the same sex has the greatest influence. This is when a child needs a model— an example of what it means to be a man or a woman—to begin the patterning stage for adulthood, although the parent of the opposite sex is still important. During this stage a person matures in his or her sex-role identity. Positive reactions of the opposite-sex parent to the child's attempts to become like Mum or Dad are needed to confirm and reinforce the child's developing sex-role identity.

When we were born, we did not have a self-image. It developed slowly, daily, as we internalized the atmosphere and attitudes around us. A good self-image comes from the quality of relationships between us and those individuals who played significant roles in our early lives.

Parents are intended to be God's gift

Before I was married, I used to spend a lot of time at Paula's home. She had the most beautiful parents. She never heard her parents argue or her father raise his voice to her mother. I used to say, 'God, why couldn't I have had parents like that, who love each other?' Not only do I not remember my father hugging me, I never saw him hug my mother.

My mother wasn't just overweight. Because of a glandular condition, she was obese. As a result, I always saw myself as being fat when I wasn't. I saw my dad as the town alcoholic. Although there were some wonderful times too, our family life was overshadowed by a succession of trials, tribulations and heartaches.

I used to envy Paula and her family, until a few years ago when I realized that God had chosen my parents. I began to see that He permitted the characteristics I received from them. Even in a sin-sick world, I realized it was God who made me what I am and who used my parents to mould me.

That realization kept me going while my biography was being written a few years later. At first I was scared stiff to think of some people knowing parts of my background. My wife even said, 'Dear, are you sure you want people to read this?' 'No,' I said, 'but it's too late now!'

It was an agonizing experience to have Joe Musser delve into my past in order to write my life story. He brought up a lot of hurts I hadn't dealt with. But in the long run it helped me. Now I am able to say to my heavenly Father, 'Thank you for my earthly parents.'

God takes all the circumstances of our lives, comforts us in those situations and then uses their hurts and pains to enable us to minister to others (2 Cor 1:3–4). God used Romans 8:28, 'And we know that in all things God works for the good of those who love him, who have been called according to his purpose,' to help me get a better picture of my father. I am thankful even for an alcoholic father because of God's faithfulness to use those circumstances to enable me to help others.

Perhaps you too are coming to understand some of your parents' failures more clearly. If you are, you need to come to the point of saying, 'Thank you, God, for my parents. I don't understand all of my childhood, but I trust that You will cause all of it to work together for good.'

Building a better self-image

5

List the personal characteristics that you believe made your father and mother (or could have made them) good parents.

_____

_____

_____

_____

_____

As you evaluate your parents' love, did they give you a good image of God the Father? _____ Is God like your earthly parents? _____

Name some people whose lives have helped you sense what God is like.

_____

_____

_____

_____

6

Stories of Childhood

To be thankful for our parents, no matter how poor their parenting was, is one thing. Overcoming that parenting while still using its effects for God's glory is another. By His grace, it can be done. To give you hope that your self-image can change, let me tell you about my own background and that of O'Neill, a friend of mine.

O'Neill's story

O'Neill was raised in a small town in north-east Texas by parents who were as good as gold and who loved him to the greatest of their ability to love. But for O'Neill it wasn't enough.

Because his father suffered from a poor self-image, he tried to overcome this with hard work. A self-made man who had overcome great odds in his childhood, O'Neill's father could communicate love only by giving to his family materially. He never put his arm round O'Neill. He never told him that he loved him or was proud of him.

O'Neill's mother was a woman who yearned for intimacy. O'Neill doesn't believe she ever found it. Before her death she tried to bury her hungry heart in a flurry of activities—church, girl's club and other community activities—that demanded all her time. She was lonely and fearful. Because of her fears, she was dominating, controlling and possessive.

As the oldest of three children in this not-very-close family, O'Neill worked to gain his parents' acceptance, love and approval by being what they wanted him to be. He was the obedient, good, successful son who was prominently displayed before his younger brother and sister as an example. (As a result, his brother resents him still.)

Privately, O'Neill's life was a painful one. As a 'mummy's boy', he wasn't allowed to fight with the children in the neighbourhood; Mum always intervened. By the time he reached secondary school O'Neill was the school sissy. One fellow delighted in tormenting him every morning, daring him to fight, pushing him around and harassing him to tears. He was the dread of O'Neill's life, as another boy had been at junior school. O'Neill couldn't run away yet he was too afraid to fight. He had no confidence in his ability to take care of himself. His classmates decided he was such a sissy that he must wear lace on his underwear. The nickname 'Lacy' became a taunt that tormented him for years.

To make matters worse, O'Neill had a secret fear that someone might find out he was a chronic bed-wetter. Until the age of fifteen he could never spend the night at a friend's home, which made his loneliness and sense of inferiority even worse.

His father couldn't understand the bed-wetting. He reacted to it with anger, as if O'Neill purposely wet the bed to spite him.

The teasing, bed-wetting and normal teenage problems made his early years painful. With no close friends, O'Neill tried the Scouts. But the teasing followed him there. He was consumed with fear and lack of respect for himself. He was filled with rage and had no way to express it.

Then he came across American football, and his athletic abilities developed. Gifted with a large physique and good abilities, and protected from too much hurt by all the padding on his uniform, O'Neill was encouraged to strike his opponents to the ground. By his later years at secondary school his anger at others was paying off, and he made the first team. From then on, he began to receive some respect from his classmates. He was learning to respect himself.

Eventually O'Neill outgrew the bed-wetting problem, and life began to look brighter. In his last year at school the team went to the state finals. O'Neill didn't receive any honours, however. The man who promoted athletic honours in that area didn't like O'Neill's father. Of course that hurt the son a lot. And he never managed to live down the nickname 'Lacy'.

But also in his teenage years he found a safe place to develop. The church youth group became important to him. In church O'Neill found he could be 'a big fish in a little pond'. He became leader of the young people's group, earning acclaim from the adults. He was even elected to a district office for the denomination's youth group. One summer at church camp he committed his life to full-time Christian service.

O'Neill's college career began with a jolt. A coach at a major university had said he would give him a football scholarship to pay his way through college. When signing time came, however, that coach decided not to give him one, saying he wasn't good enough to play.

Angry, O'Neill determined to prove to the coach and to himself that he could play football at a major university. Enrolling without the scholarship, he began the job of proving himself athletically. In the spring of his first year O'Neill made the team, received a scholarship and moved into the athletic dorm.

The head coach, however, didn't like him. O'Neill didn't smoke or drink; he trained all year round and was known as a nice guy. The coach harassed him on and off the field, made false accusations about him, kept him and several teammates out of the game, told him he would never play another game of football with him, didn't grant him an award even though he had earned it and conveniently forgot to order his senior awards. The pain was almost more than O'Neill could bear, but he thought of his dad's philosophy, 'If he can live with it, I can live without it!'

O'Neill's weekends at college were times of great loneliness and depression. At times his rage caused him to sink into almost suicidal depression. He would get in his car and cruise round town looking for a girl to pick up or a fight to get into. All the time he continued to prepare himself for the ministry, even though he knew there was no reality to his Christian experience. After a while his conduct in college earned him a new nickname from teammates, 'Preacher'.

O'Neill still had no intimate friends. He was afraid to let anyone know the small, frightened boy he was inside. He was certain no one could like him, because he certainly didn't like himself. Again he was a solitary, quietly suffering person.

The summer after his first year at college O'Neill heard the gospel of Christ for the first time. If it had been preached in his home church, he hadn't heard it. He accepted Christ with expectations that now at last his life would be completely transformed. Yet nothing seemed to change. His loneliness and sense of inferiority and rage didn't go away. As a result, he was more miserable than before. He knew that Christ was in his life, but his life wasn't all that different.

During his final year O'Neill met his wife, and they were married between terms. Marriage brought out O'Neill's personal inferiority feelings even more. He couldn't communicate because he was afraid to let her know him. Their marriage simply drifted along.

After college they were hired to work at a Christian camp in California. That summer became a significant turning point in O'Neill's life. At camp he met a Christian counsellor who gave him hope that he could be different. After one brief afternoon session, O'Neill's life began to change dramatically.

Since that summer the years have been a drama of how God has worked to heal him of his pain, loneliness, anger and feelings of inferiority. He has spent many hours trying to understand himself. He has prayed, studied the Scriptures and sought counselling from many people. His wife and he have spent many hours in personal therapy. At times the struggle was almost overwhelming, but today O'Neill is not the person you have just read about. He is different. His self-image has been and is being transformed.

Today he carries no bitterness, although the pain of his childhood can still make him cry. He has grown through most of those hurts and can honestly say he is thankful for the pain he suffered. Its result has been an ability to minister to hundreds of other hurting people over the years.

'Praise be to the God and Father of our Lord Jesus Christ, the Father of compassion and the God of all comfort, who comforts us in all our troubles, so that we can comfort those in any trouble with the comfort we ourselves have received from God.'[1]

Josh's remembrances

My folks finished school at the age of seven. In the small town in which I grew up, if my English teachers emphasized correct grammar, it never got through to me. As a result, when it came to correct English, I didn't know a thing. I never learnt what a 'double negative' was. I didn't know you were supposed to use a single verb with a single subject: 'They *is* going' was good enough for me during my upbringing.

At infant school, Mrs Duel tried to switch me from being lefthanded to using my right hand. I would have to sit at a table while she said, 'Build a house out of blocks.' If I reached out with my left hand, instantly she would hit it with a ruler and say, 'Stop, think it through. Do it with your right hand.' The experience caused a speech impediment.

Every time I got scared, nervous or tired, usually at school, I would stutter. Eventually my internal response to Mrs Duel's efforts became, 'Build your own stupid house, you silly lady!'

At our equivalent of middle school, I was supposed to recite Abraham Lincoln's Gettysburg Address. In front of everyone, Mr Elliott said, 'Say it, say it! Stop stuttering and say it!' I got up and ran out of the room crying in front of all my friends.

During my brother's visits home from college, he would constantly correct my speech. I was embarrassed to open my mouth when he was around. I thought he was trying to put me down. I never realized that the torment he was causing me was meant for my own benefit.

Added to this was my father's alcoholism. My friends would come to school and joke about my dad being drunk. They never knew how much their jokes bothered me. Outwardly I would laugh, but I was crying on the inside.

Sometimes I would go out to the barn and find my mother lying in the manure behind the cows, knocked down so hard by my dad that she couldn't get up. Twice she left home.

When we had friends round, I would take my father out, tie him up in the barn and park the car on the far side of the silo. We would tell our friends he'd had to go somewhere.

I don't think anyone could have hated another person more than I hated my father. Several times, exploding in rage, I nearly killed him.

Talk about self-image. I was allergic to myself!

To compensate for my weaknesses and to try to please the tormentors in my life, I worked harder than everyone else at chores, studies and athletics. As a result, I excelled in studies and at sports, all the while expecting to fail in both areas.

When I entered college, my home grammar caught up with me. It was so poor that I was told I was a lowest grade student. I became embarrassed to speak up in class. I remember a time at the first-year English class when the professor asked, 'Where's Bob?' I spoke up saying, 'He doesn't feel good.' In front of everyone, Dr Hampton said, 'Mr McDowell, he doesn't feel *well*.' I looked at her totally perplexed. I didn't know the difference between 'good' and 'well'. To me it was gooder to say good!

Then a professor told me I had two things going for me. The first was the ability to put arguments and facts together to prove a point. The second was a tremendous determination and drive. He suggested I consider going into law. As I saw hope for a life in which people would respect me, my mind went beyond that possibility. I mapped out a strategy that would carry me all the way to becoming the governor of Michigan in twenty-five years. Step number one was to be elected first-year representative for my class, which I soon ticked off my list as accomplished.

With my newly discovered powers of logic, I chose to refute Christianity for a term project, because of an unsatisfying encounter I'd had with an evangelistic group. Soon after starting the project, I ran into a group of Christian students. For more than a year I argued about the truth of Christianity with them. After looking into the evidence thoroughly, however, I realized I couldn't disprove it.

But still I held out. Even if Jesus did perform miracles and was raised from the dead, He seemed like a spoilsport to me. I didn't want anyone to ruin my good times. More than a year later, after tossing and turning all one night thinking about it, I gave in. I told God, 'In spite of myself, I guess I believe You're real.' I admitted to Him I'd been wrong—sinful—and asked Him to forgive me. I told Him to take my life and make it more like those of my Christian friends.

At first I didn't feel any better. I felt worse, in fact, wondering what I had been dragged into. I wondered if I had really gone off the deep end. But in six to eighteen months I found that my life was changing. A kind of mental peace began to take the place of my constant restlessness. My explosive temper disappeared. I used to blow my top if someone just looked at me cross-eyed. During my first year at college, I had almost killed a man. I didn't try to change my temper. I just found it had gone one day when I ran into a situation that would normally have caused a big blow-up.

However, there were still weaknesses to overcome. But step by step, sometimes by giant steps, they too changed. When I changed to Wheaton College, a Christian college, I struggled over a challenge to give everything I had to the Lord. I didn't want to, because I thought He might want me to go into Christian ministry, which meant only one thing to me—speaking. At the time my bad grammar and stammering were still so evident that I thought my giving 'everything' to Him was mighty little.

Finally I said, 'God, I don't think I've got any speaking talents; I don't have any gifts. [In reality I did, but I didn't think so.] I stutter when I'm scared, I speak horrible English. Look, here are all my limitations, so You can't possibly want me in a ministry. But if You can take these limitations and make something out of them, then I'll serve You the rest of my life.'

In the hands of a God without limitations, those very weaknesses have become strengths, giving me opportunity to speak about Him to millions of people in half the countries of the world. I'm convinced that I now live a supernatural life, a life that is beyond my limitations, because of God's reality in it.

Of course, my speeches are still filled with incorrect grammar. Every time I open my mouth, I'm aware of my weaknesses and the grace of God. But I'm also aware that He does make the difference. Because of that, I can honestly say, 'Thank You, God, for giving me my childhood and my parents.' If it hadn't been for them, I wouldn't be much of what I am today.

And I am 'confident of this, that he who began a good work [in me] will carry it on to completion until the day of Christ Jesus.'[2]

Building
a better self-image

6

Consider the adage, 'I'm not what I ought—or was made—to be, but, thank God, I'm not what I used to be and, by the grace of God, I'm not what I will be.' Then consider specifically how this might apply to you.

List five ways in which you are not what you ought, or were made, to be.

_____

_____

_____

List five ways for which you can thank God that you are not what you used to be.

_____

_____

_____

List five characteristics which, by the grace of God, you hope, and even expect, to manifest in the future.

_____

_____

_____

7

The Case of the Vanishing Father

Researchers predict that by 1990 one out of four children in the United States will be living with one parent and that parent, almost always, will be the mother. That trend has been in evidence for a number of years.

An even greater number of children, however, like the two you've just read about, are affected by a Dad who is physically present in the home—at least he sleeps there—but who is distant, passive, unaffectionate, rejecting and who spends little time with his children. It's like putting children in a sweet shop, but not letting them satisfy the desire for sweets that is created when they see sweets in front of them.

In an article for *McCall's* (an American women's magazine) entitled 'The Vanishing American Father', Max Lerner wrote that the changing role and influence of the father was an issue of tremendous significance:

> The vanishing father is perhaps the central fact of the changing American family structure today. His virtual disappearance holds important consequences for his wife and his daughters, but I believe that its most critical impact is upon his sons.[1]

The late Dr Paul Popenoe, formerly director of the American Institute of Family Relations, in an article entitled 'Why Are Fathers Failures?' made an even stronger statement. He wrote, 'The idea...that children of either sex can get along satisfactorily, in a two-sexed world, with the patterns furnished them by only one sex is distinctly harmful. They need the patterns of both sexes from infancy onward.'[2]

In 1960, in the United States the number of children living with one parent was less than one in ten. In 1978 it was nearly one in five. And, as we've seen, those ratios are expected to narrow still further.

Such statistics are alarming. Millions more children will not have the balanced influence of both male and female parent figures. Problems will result in the lives of these children and in the adults they will become. The emotional scars they carry will affect their personal lives, their marriages and the types of parents they in turn will be.

A friend of mine became aware of how this father-child breakdown causes personality problems when he was personnel director for Campus Crusade for Christ. In that position he interviewed college graduates for Campus Crusade staff positions. He observed that women applicants consistently manifested a healthier, more confident self-image and sense of their sexual identity than did male applicants. Taken as a whole, the men showed weaker self-images and a poor sense of masculinity. All of the applicants were considered outstanding, the cream of the crop: college club leaders, student body officers, top athletes, outstanding scholars. Yet the men were consistently less confident than the women in sex-role identity and self-image.

The missing father's effect on boys

Traditionally in our culture a young girl has a mother figure at home as a role-model during the same-sex state of parental influence (puberty to adulthood). During those years, girls usually have a closer relationship with their female role-model than boys have with their male role-model. Often the father figure is rarely available or is totally removed from his sons' lives. Because of a closer relationship to their parental role-model, girls tend to develop healthier views of themselves.

If I had magical powers to change one cultural phenomena, it would be to correct the problem of the absentee, passive or non-involved father. No problem, I believe, has affected our society more than this one.

Harold M. Voth, MD, senior psychiatrist and psychoanalyst at the Menninger Foundation in Topeka, Kansas, says this in his book, *The Castrated Family:*

> Far-reaching and serious consequences result when internal family arrangements deviate from the norm. Virtually every patient I have personally treated, or whose treatment I have supervised, or whose treatment I have studied through a research endeavor, has revealed an aberrant family constellation. The most common pattern was the family in which the mother was domineering and aggressive and the father weak and passive. Some of these fathers were aggressive and assertive in their work situations but timid and weak in relation to their wives. The wives in these marriages clearly 'wore the pants.'
>
> Another pattern was that of a weak mother who tended to cling to her children, and a tyrannical father who was dictatorial but incapable of experiencing closeness to his wife or children. While it may seem that such a father is head of the family, actually much of the responsibility and authority falls to the wife except for periods when the father makes his presence felt by angry, usually irrational, outbursts. Some women are forced to fill the role of both mother and father by necessity. These women may be feminine but the absence of the father places all of the responsibilities on them; the effects of this family pattern on children as well as on themselves are not good. Fathers and mothers may be hostile, rejecting, overly anxious, or possessive. Some families lack any semblance of an authority structure. Some parents live up to their responsibilities sporadically.

All of these conditions within the family adversely affect the child's personality development.

Strong fathers and strong mothers (in the feminine sense— strong femininity is not aggressiveness), who love each other, who cooperate with each other, and whose roles are clearly defined, produce healthy children. When this pattern is disturbed in any of a number of ways, emotional disturbances of a wide variety are the result in the children.[3]

The industrial revolution and fatherhood

The problem, it seems, began with the industrial revolution and the urbanization of society. As long as we had an agrarian, rural culture, the father figure was an important and dynamic factor in the home life and in child development. Since his work and career centred on the home, there was greater contact with the children, particularly since they usually worked alongside him. The lack of outside distractions, such as television, usually meant that evenings were more family centred and children were together with their father.

Today a father usually works away from home, and children rarely see his workplace. Often they don't know what he does. The children may have contact with him at breakfast or dinner, but sometimes they have neither. Some fathers travel all week and collapse all weekend. They are almost nonentities when it comes to their children's lives. Recent research indicates that the average American father spends less than six minutes a week in quality interaction with his children.

Children without effective mother relationships are fewer in number; yet mother-deprived children in our society have a greater number of substitute, female authority-figures to which they can attach themselves than do father-deprived children. Substitute mothers can be found teaching Sunday school and primary school classes, leading Cub Scouts and even athletic groups.

To one degree or another the huge majority of people in America today have been touched by the problem of an ineffective father-relationship. It is an epidemic with many causes and far-reaching consequences.

Consequences for women

The symptoms we see in girls and women from homes with ineffective fathers are numerous. The more obvious ones often cause the greatest difficulty. Daughters are affected most in the opposite-sex stage of parental influence (age three to puberty). Although there are also consequences in their adolescent years, effects from the pre-puberty stage of influence seem to be the more significant.

When a young girl does not have a warm, loving, touching, affectionate relationship with her father during pre-school and infant school years, she may become a woman with a basic distrust of men built into her personality. She may not be conscious of the cause of this distrust or even of its degree, but it is there. It has its roots in her relationship with her father, but it is displaced to (placed on) other men in her life.

A second problem women often demonstrate is the problem of hostility towards men. Again, the problem has its roots in deep bitterness towards her father for not meeting her needs as a little girl. This hostility may be unconscious but, like the distrust, it too is displaced to other males in her life.

A third problem is the resulting need for affection and attention from men. The lack of a warm, affectionate relationship with her father during the heterosexual stage may leave a woman with an almost insatiable desire to be held and to receive affection from a man.

Relating to hubby as Daddy

Another problem is a consequence of the first three. Such women often have marital and sexual problems that they don't understand or don't seem able to control. A common marital problem is that of a woman relating emotionally to her husband as if he were her father. In every marriage there is some transference of emotions to a mate that were originally intended for the person's parent of the opposite sex. This presents particular problems in marriages where the wife has come from a home with an ineffective father. She relates to her husband emotionally as if he were Daddy, seeking to have her husband meet the emotional needs that were never met by her father.

This transference of emotions can be particularly damaging in the sexual aspect of marriage. Counsellors report that some women say that their emotions about having sex with their husband are those of repulsion, similar to the emotions they would feel should their fathers approach them sexually. Not having had their needs met for non-erotic, fatherly affection, they may unconsciously be responding to their mate's physical affection as they would should affection from their fathers turn to sexual foreplay. These women, it seems, displace their paternal distrust and hostility to their husbands, which makes it very difficult for them to respond sexually.

Before marriage, counsellors report further, some of these women were promiscuous in their attempts to have their needs for affection met. Before marriage, with no sense of total or lifelong commitment, their desires for affection and attention caused them to be sexually free, but after entering the marriage bond, their father-directed distrust and hostility shuts off their freedom.

Extremely promiscuous women have acknowledged that it was not the sex act itself that enticed them; it was their hunger for affection. Many say that they gave their bodies only in order to get the affection they craved.

Thus, the childhood need for fatherly affection is the root cause behind the sexual promiscuity of many young women today. Usually girls who have experienced good, close relationships with their fathers in their home environment are able to maintain better control and avoid problems with promiscuity.

Consequences for men

The lack of a warm, loving affectionate father-figure likewise has great impact on a boy's life. The impact is felt during the same-sex stage of parental influence, beginning at puberty, when boys most need a male authority figure as a role model.

A boy with an ineffective father relationship grows up with a poor sense of masculinity. He has little confidence in himself as a male human being. Since he lacked an effective relationship with his dad, it is difficult for him to know how to 'be a man'.

Most men rarely, if ever, let anyone see this sense of inadequacy in their lives. Many of them feel they have to wear a mask of confidence continually. When life crumbles in on them and they are forced into counselling, then the counsellor (but usually only the counsellor) hears them admit their true needs.

Proving one's masculinity

The result of this poor sense of masculinity is that insecure males often set out to prove to themselves and the world that they are really men. In hundreds of ways they strive to convince themselves and others that they are masculine. They are vulnerable to the 'macho myths' that permeate our society. Real men are rugged, unemotional, performance-oriented individualists who are always in control. Big boys don't cry.

In order to make them feel more confident of their ability to live up to such a myth they generally strive much more for status symbols, titles and degrees than do women. They strive to prove their masculinity through achievements or accomplishments, particularly in the material realm. If I make more money or accomplish more goals than other men, I must be 'a better man' than the average Joe. One-to-one competition is also used to prove their masculinity. If I beat you, whether at draughts or football, the winner is obviously 'the better man'. (For me, childhood competitions were a very significant issue.) Some men use sexual conquests to prove their male prowess. For several decades our culture has glorified the 'James Bond type', one who is extremely successful in seduction and violent intrigue.

In the last few years, however, we have seen a trend towards advocating a more nurturing, tenderness-oriented male as the true man. Some husbands and fathers—mostly younger ones, including many Christians—are choosing to develop these qualities in their lives. This change, I believe, spells hope for a greater number of young children growing up today. In order to be as successful as possible, however, in developing nurturant qualities, these men also need to understand the results of parental deprivation in their own backgrounds.

Hostility and fear of women

A second problem often observed in the lives of men from father-deprived homes is hostility towards women. This may develop because the mother (or mother substitute) tries to compensate for the absence or passivity of the father. By the time most boys are ten or eleven, however, they've had enough mothering and are ready for more male input. The stronger, more dominant or smothering the mother is in trying to make up for the father's lack of attention, the greater becomes the boy's hostility and bitterness (even though the mother's intentions are good). Often, because the boy also admires and respects his mother very much, he develops ambivalent feelings towards her, refusing to admit his hostility and bitterness. He would never want to hurt her, but he may vow to get away from her attentions, emotionally and physically, as soon as possible. In adulthood, the boy's anger, even rage, towards his mother (like father-directed hostility and bitterness in a girl's life) are displaced to other women.

Third, a corollary to hostility towards the mother is the fear of being dominated by any woman in adult life. An adult male may vow never to allow another woman to control him. Often this is not a conscious fear, but shows up in the ways he avoids closeness or intimacy with women. To him, erotic closeness is the only intimacy that feels safe from his fear of being dominated. As a husband he may become compliant and silent, or angry and distant. He may even initiate constant physical contact in order to have the upper hand in the marital relationship. Regardless, such behaviour is designed to break the bonds of female control. They have a greater detrimental effect on marriages than most men and women realize. Few people who have this problem ever realize the extent of its effect on their marriages.

Many men relate to their wives as if she is Mum and he is a teenage son again. Some women say that their husbands are like another child, balking at taking on family or household responsibilities. To the husband, his wife's requests or reminders seem too much like his mother's, so he responds to them in the same alienated way he did as a teenager.

Problems in male friendships

A fourth problem observed in father-deprived men is a need for, but fear of, forming deep relationships with men. The father-son relationship should be a training ground, as well as a teaching model, for intimate male relationships.

Never having experienced such relationships in the home, however, most men don't know how to develop them. They also may fear that close male friendships could hint at homosexuality. Current studies indicate that most men in our society have no real friend they can share their lives with in an intimate way. Herb Goldberg in *The Hazards of Being Male* writes of the lost art of friendship. After men discuss the weather, sports, stock market, interest rates and perhaps the new sexy new secretary at work, they have nothing else to say to one another.[4]

Another problem in these issues is that of male homosexuality, which appears to be increasing at a much greater rate than lesbianism. It seems that the need for a relationship with a substitute father figure, along with fear and hostility towards women, programmes men to be susceptible to homosexuality. The desire for closeness with a father figure links itself with sexual and affectional needs, which some young males then try to meet in a gay relationship.

Some therapists, like Arthur Janov, who wrote *The Primal Scream*,[5] believe that the goal of homosexuality is heterosexuality. A man seeks to meet unmet paternal needs from childhood through homosexual relationships so he can then mature to heterosexual relationships. (The same would be true for lesbians lacking an affectionate maternal relationship in childhood.) If Janov is correct, then in days to come their should be an increasing drop-out rate in the gay community. Many such drop-outs may remain secret gays, however, for fear of losing friendships built in the gay community and fear of not being accepted as an ex-gay in normal society.

The cycle continues

Most men in today's culture have been affected to some degree by the problem of the passive, non-involved, absentee father. The problem has created a deeply engrained cycle in our culture: dominant women marry passive men and these marriages produce dominant daughters and passive sons. The cycle then begins all over again. With each generation, the problems get worse and the consequences of our poor self-concepts become more devastating. Today there is an epidemic of poor or unhealthy self-images in both men and women that can be traced to the breakdown of the parenting process.

Armand M. Nicholi, a Harvard psychiatrist, summarizes this theory:

> If any one factor influences the character development and emotional stability of an individual, it is the quality of the relationship he or she experiences as a child with both parents. Conversely, if people suffering from severe, nonorganic emotional illness have one experience in common, it is the absence of a parent through death, divorce, a time-demanding job, or for other reasons.

The discussion in this chapter has focused on the effects of father deprivation. Mother deprivation, however, which is becoming greater as more mothers carry on full-time careers outside the home, can be likewise devastating. Before families started moving so much, we could expect grandparents, aunts and uncles to take up some of the slack in effective parenting. Today few children have the security and back-up reinforcement of a large extended family.

As we move into the late twentieth century we will see a culture of more and more individuals who have been deprived of effective parenting. As both single-parent and two-career families increase, more and more children will be raised with a lack of involved parents of either sex. The scars of such deprivations will be etched deeply into the self-images of the coming generations.

I do, however, see some elements of hope. As has been said, some younger fathers, many of them Christians, are recognizing the need for effective fathering and are making it a priority in their lives. Further, the tapes, films and programmes of Dr James Dobson, a Christian child and family psychiatrist, on the importance of parenting—and of fathering in particular—have become well known in Christian and secular groups. As for myself, a travelling father of three children, I find the information in this chapter especially significant.

Building a better self-image

7

Read John 10:37–38 and John 14:7–10. Write these verses in

your own words. _____

_____

_____

_____

_____

Our heavenly Father is exactly like _____ , so we

can learn about God, our heavenly Father, by learning about _____

_____

Write a prayer telling God the Father what you believe He is like.
Be specific and free with your words. He knows your heart already,
but it helps to express thoughts and feelings in words.

_____

_____

_____

_____

_____

8

Self-Image: Resting on a Three-Legged Stool

Susan, a full-time Christian worker, found it nearly impossible to carry on her work. Fear paralysed her whenever she tried to step into the leadership roles demanded of her position. She was convinced that her job would be taken from her if her past were discovered.

A counsellor spent several sessions with Susan before she was able to admit what her past activities were, they so repulsed her now. Finally, from her deep hurt, fear and anguish, it all spilled out: her numerous affairs, her abortion, her homosexual involvement.

Even though her life had changed dramatically since she became a Christian, Susan still suffered from a poor self-image because of those past sins and not knowing how to deal with them. The consequences of her negative view of herself were obvious. Her problem couldn't be solved by a surgeon who could remove a diseased self-image as might be done with an appendix or gallbladder.

Our self-image is a part of us that is different from an organ. If you were to study a medical textbook, you would find diagrams, illustrations and even photographs of your internal organs, both normal and abnormal ones. Such graphics enable medical students to have a better understanding of the structure and function of the human body. But someone's self-image can't be photographed. Because it has no shape, we are more limited in our means of understanding it. We can, however, attempt to describe some of its components.

Three basic emotional needs are common to all persons. These are:

1. The need to feel loved, accepted; to have a sense of belonging.
2. The need to feel acceptable; to have a sense of worthiness.
3. The need to feel adequate; to have a sense of competence.

Such needs appear to be foundational in every personality. They serve as three pillars around which the input from our childhood is structured and our self-image is developed. Those pillars—belonging, worthiness and competence—are the supports on which a healthy self-image rests. If one pillar is underdeveloped or damaged, a person's entire self-image is lopsided, unstable and shaky.[1]

Picture your self-image as resembling a three-legged stool. The stool seat, on which someone sits and rests all his weight, is supported by three equal but separate legs. It doesn't take much imagination to picture what happens to a person who tries to use a stool with one leg broken or too short.

The stronger the pillars of our self-image, the more they will withstand trauma in later life. (Even the healthiest of adult self-images can be shaken by severe tragedy or trauma, however, forcing a person to lean on someone or something else.)

A sense of belonging

As a toddler Linda had been abandoned at a stranger's front door. Early deprivation left her self-image with a fragile quality that was readily apparent. The basic pillar to a healthy self-image is a sense of belonging or a feeling of being loved. It's the sense of security a person feels when he or she is accepted by other people, a feeling of being part of a relationship, loved by at least one other person. It's the knowledge that someone 'really cares for me'. Belonging is what I feel when I know I am loved *unconditionally*, just as I am.

> *The basic pillar to a healthy self-image is a sense of belongingness or a feeling of being loved.*

The world is full of people like Linda who have never experienced adequate unconditional love and acceptance. Of course, just about everyone has experienced some love. But no one has experienced from a human source the unconditional love and acceptance necessary to remove all fragility from our self-image. To one degree or another the love all of us received was imperfect, because the people loving us weren't perfect. At the very least, we all occasionally experienced a conditional love and acceptance that communicated, 'I love you because...' That kind of love carries an unspoken and perhaps unconscious threat. We hear, 'I love you because you're so _____' The threat we feel, perhaps without knowing it, is 'What happens if I stop being _____?'

Conditional love leaves our basic love-hunger unsatisfied and our sense of belonging inadequately developed. Most of us grow up with this pillar or leg on our self-image stool somewhat shaky. Others have a stronger belonging pillar, but still it is not totally stable.

James D. Mallory and Stanley C. Baldwin in *The Kink and I* introduce a chapter on love with this comment: 'Love is the most powerful healing force that can exist in an individual's life.'[2] Psychological research has demonstrated that the single most important factor in developing a healthy personality is the sense of being loved and cared for and then being able to love others.

A sense of worthiness

Belonging is the sense of being acceptable to others. Related to it is a sense of worthiness, a feeling of being acceptable to yourself. If you are acceptable to others, you will more likely feel acceptable to yourself. Belonging deals with a sense of security. Worthiness deals with being whole on the inside, having a good feeling about yourself, a feeling of 'I like myself; I respect myself; I am not ashamed of the way I treat myself.' It's a feeling of being OK, clean, right and proper. It's the feeling that I'm good enough or worthy of other persons' acceptance. I am worthy of being loved.

Most children, as they grow up, idealize their mothers and fathers. They place them on a pedestal, seeing them as perfect. Mum and Dad can do no wrong. Then, when children who have idealized their mothers and fathers don't experience the unconditional love and acceptance they want, they assume that the problem lies within themselves. Unconsciously they reason, 'Mother and Dad are perfect, so obviously they would love me if I were worthy of their love.' What registers in their young minds is, 'I'm not good enough to be loved.' Some children can verbalize these feelings at an early age. Many others are unable to verbalize such insights even as adults, yet they try to compensate for their feelings of unworthiness through their adult accomplishments.

Jim, for instance, has reached the pinnacle of success in his profession. He writes many books, lectures around the world, drives an expensive sports car and lives in a large suburban home. He has job security and all his peers view him as extremely successful. Yet when you get to know him well, you can see Jim's fear and insecurity. To close friends he admits his deep-rooted, poor self-esteem. Tormented by feelings of inferiority, he doesn't feel worthy to be loved.

The world is full of people who feel unworthy to one degree or another. Experiences from childhood relationships often leave deep wounds that are re-opened or worsened by teenage and adult experiences. Sometimes our sense of unworthiness has been magnified by our engaging in activities that have violated personal standards and left a feeling of guilt. Often we are ashamed of the way we have treated others or ourselves.

All of those experiences and feelings are related to our sense of worthiness. A healthy self-image demands a strong worthiness pillar. To the degree that our sense of worth is damaged or inadequate, to that degree our self-image is unstable.

A sense of competence

The third pillar of our self-image is an inner sense of competence. 'I can do it!' is the confident attitude of persons with healthy self-images when they approach a new task. This optimistic outlook inspires them with hopefulness and courage. It is closely related to their success in solving past problems. Persons with a healthy sense of competence don't face each new day with fear but with joy and enthusiasm for the opportunities that lie ahead.

Many people read to their children the classic children's story, 'The Little Engine That Could.' It tells the story of a train engine that had to pull a heavy load up a mountain. All the big engines told him he couldn't do it, but as he strained under the load, he kept saying to himself, 'I think I can, I think I can.' As a result, despite all the bigger engines' doubts, he reached the top of the mountain.

As children grow and are allowed to explore and venture out from Mum and Dad, they begin to build a healthy sense of competence. As they are encouraged to try to accomplish new things and to work to overcome difficulties, their sense of confidence in their abilities grows. As they try new things with more and more success, and as they learn to pick themselves up again and again after setbacks, they learn to say, 'I can do it!'

Watch young babies as they learn to walk. They take a step or two and fall down. In time they take many steps. Observe their joy as Mum and Dad praise this new accomplishment. Soon they walk everywhere and begin to run after big brother or sister. They develop a growing sense of competence as they learn other skills.

Parents play an important role in helping children learn to feel competent. As they allow them to try new and more difficult tasks, they communicate their belief that the child is capable of accomplishing them. When parents don't let a child take risks, try new things and explore new areas, they communicate, knowingly or not, a lack of confidence in the child, an attitude of 'I don't think you're capable of doing new things.' As children we needed our parents' encouragement and help in order to develop a sense of competence. The child who is sheltered and not allowed to take risks grows up with an underdeveloped sense of competence.

Amanda is an attractive young woman in her twenties who suffers from a poor self-image. Much of her problem originated in childhood competition between her and her sister, Mary. Mary always seemed to make her parents happy, while Amanda felt she never made them happy. The conclusion Amanda reached was that she was unlovable. Since she couldn't make her parents happy and Mary could, she decided that the problem was her fault.

Today Amanda's evaluation of herself is the same. She still believes she is unlovable. Further, her entire life is organized round trying to disprove what she believes to be true.

Amanda needs someone with an authority equal to that of her parents during her childhood to give her a new appraisal of her worth. The new statement of Amanda's worth must be based on her true value as a person. Ideally, this appraisal will be God's view of her. Amanda then must revise her self-evaluation based on His appraisal of her value.

Every person, Christian or non-Christian, needs these pillars developed adequately. Each of them is of equal importance in developing a healthy self-image. In our culture people often try to compensate for a weak sense of belonging or worthiness with an overdeveloped sense of competence. They may become workaholics out of a mistaken notion that, if they accomplish enough, they will be worthy and then people will love them. Or like Amanda they may organize their whole lives round the idea of doing something to become lovable.

Just as a farmer is ill at ease sitting on a three-legged milk stool with uneven legs, so people have trouble being at peace within themselves with three uneven pillars to their self-images. Individuals without balance among their sense of worth, belonging and competence will always be striving to stabilize their image of themselves. Ideally, with strong, balanced legs to their self-images, people can relax, enjoy being themselves, feel good about who they are and find the joy that life has to offer.

Building a better self-image

8

Do you recall what Paul wrote about our intrinsic worth? 'I want you to realize that God has been made rich because we who are Christ's have been given to him' (Eph 1:18, LB). From that verse, see if your answers to the following questions are the same as those provided here.

According to Ephesians 1:18, who was made rich? 'God was.'

How do you make someone rich? 'You give them something of value.'

What of value was given to God to make Him rich? 'I was!'

Does this mean that God is richer because He has you? (Answer yes or no.) _____

Does this mean that you are of value to God? (Answer yes or no.) _____

9

Restructuring the Foundation

What difference should it make in your self-image that you are a Christian? Up to this point, most of what has been said about self-image is true of every living person. Every one of us has participated in the process of being parented. We all—Christians and non-Christians alike—have the pillars of belongingness, worthiness, and competence on which to support our self-images. You don't have to be a Christian to have a good self-image.

A person's Christian commitment does make a difference, however, ideally a visible one. What a tragedy that some Christians never allow their faith to penetrate deeply enough into their personality to heal and change their self-image.

When I trusted Christ to be my Saviour, my self-image was not automatically transformed. I didn't have immediate victory over the deep scars of my past, even though through trusting Christ I received the potential, the Holy Spirit, for healing those wounds and transforming my self-image. It took a growth process for me to make substantial progress towards thinking and becoming like Christ. The changes I see in myself now seem almost unbelievable when I look back to the person I used to be. Yet, after all these years, not everything is smoothed out in my life. The growth process still continues—and will until I die. The same is true of you.

Paul tells us, 'If anyone is in Christ, he is a new creation; the old has gone, the new has come!'[1] When a person accepts Christ, he becomes a new creature, and the process of that being manifested in one's daily experience begins.

If you're like me, you have wished that some old things would have changed that didn't. I still have the same personal history from my childhood, the same parents, the same brother, the same experiences.

Factors that didn't change are ones that influenced the formation of my self-image, so it's no wonder that my self-concept didn't change right away. It was almost the same immediately after conversion as it had been before.

The 'new things' Paul talked about were spiritual—internal changes that began to affect me as I started to grow spiritually in the weeks and months after my conversion. Most people's experiences of being 'born again' are similar in that regard. Only a few have the immediate dramatic changes we seem to hear about so often.

Peeling off old garments

Jesus said, 'Lazarus, come forth!' and upon His command, a corpse became alive. Lazarus had been dead four days and was wearing the garments of death, linen body wrappings soaked in spices to help preserve the dead body. Nevertheless, new life went right through those grave clothes and into that body.

Lazarus didn't need his death garments any more. As he tried to walk out of the tomb, however, he found the going tough. He was still wrapped in all that clothing. Nonetheless, a revitalized Lazarus managed to shuffle his way to the door. Then Jesus told the former mourners, 'Take off the grave clothes and let him go.' With the help of his friends, Lazarus was set free to experience his new life.

When Lazarus received his new life, the bonds of the grave wrappings didn't break instantaneously. It was a process. The wrappings had to be peeled and ripped off with the help of others.

As newborn Christians we too have new life. But the grave wrappings of an unhealthy self-image, left over from our previous state, often hamper our ability to function freely in this new life. Our experience in Christ is a process of having the wrappings of an inadequate self-image unwound, with the help of others, giving us more and more freedom to activate all the potential of new life in Christ.

The process of maturity

Have you ever wished that God would transform you into a mature Christian instantaneously? At times, immediate maturity has seemed far preferable to all the pain and suffering that are so often a part of our personal growth. Yet God puts us through experiences that demand a maturing process. We often forget that the apostle Paul, already a religious leader before his conversion, spent fourteen years in a process of spiritual growth before he began his missionary journeys and writings. There is no maturing without this process.

We all are engaged in this process of growth, which includes the area of our self-image. Through our relationship with God, we come to see the way He views us. Our awareness of that reality becomes a stable foundation on which our self-image can rest and develop. That new foundation in turn gives us a sense of worth, security and hope that we could receive no other way. Each pillar of our self-concept is being reinforced, transformed and made secure on the new foundation of our Christian experiences.

This transformation is not just a reinforcing of the old pillars of our self-concept, but a rebuilding of them. The process involves more than just taking an old pillar and standing it on a new foundation. Part of it requires gaining insights from our new experiences in Christian growth to change the outlooks we have had on experiences from our old personal history. These new outlooks can then produce not only a healing but a rebuilding of each pillar of our self-image.

Turning over old bricks

Christian transformation then is not just a reinforcing of the old pillars, but a *restructuring* of them. It's like taking all the bricks out of a haphazardly built pillar, turning them over, viewing them anew and seeing for the first time where they fit best. Then we can place them in the pillar correctly, as they were meant to be placed, realizing that every brick has a proper place in the make-up of the pillar. Instead of each brick of experience sticking out of the pillar at odd angles, with seemingly no purpose or little effect on making the pillar stable, a builder's *level*—the Word of God—is used to put each brick of experience in the spot that will best bolster the bricks beside it. The Holy Spirit then becomes the new mortar that holds the brick firmly, snugly, in its proper place.

> *The truest thing about*
> *ourselves is what the Bible says.*

Viewing reality the right way up

Through studying the book of Romans, we come to realize that the truest thing about ourselves is what the Bible says. We find out if what *we* think about *us* doesn't agree with that, then we're living in fantasy. Our five senses can mislead us.

It's like flying in a storm where you can't see the horizon. You may be flying upside down but your five senses are likely to tell you you're flying the right way up. Pilots call this sensation *vertigo*. Everything they see, feel, hear, touch and taste may tell them they're the right way up, but if their instruments tell them they're upside down, they know that the truest thing about their situation is what those instruments say. Pilots have to learn to trust their instruments, not their senses.

Often we experience what could be called 'spiritual vertigo'. In other words, our emotions, feelings and five senses tell us one thing, but the Word of God tells us the opposite is true.

> *A healthy self-image is being*
> *committed to the truth of*
> *God's estimation of you.*

Our instrument is the Word of God, but sometimes we don't use it. Sometimes we feel we're not forgiven by God, we're condemned, or we're here and God is off somewhere in Outer Mongolia. But all the time, because of what the Bible says about us, we can still know that we're children of God. We learn that as we place our trust in what our instrument, the Word of God, says about us, our lives level out and we start to go forward again. A healthy self-image is being committed to the truth of God's estimation of you.

But you have to have the biblical picture of who and what you are in Christ before you can start responding correctly to what otherwise seems to be a topsy-turvy world. It's like what happened when a fellow bought a birthday gift for a friend who loves to put puzzles together. He bought two picture puzzles and, as a joke, switched the box tops. The guy who received them became totally frustrated, as he tried to put together a puzzle that he thought should look like the box top.

We need to stop using only feelings and attitudes about ourselves as the 'box-top picture' of who we are. The Word of God is the true picture to go by. Once you get a good look at that, then you can begin working to fit together all the little pieces of your life to make up the correct image of who you are, the design for which appears in God's Word.

So often one's attitudes are developed and decisions are made on wrong assumptions or information. We base our attitudes on what we think God thinks about us and not on what He actually thinks about us, which is revealed in His Word. The truth of Scripture about *you* and about *me* is the starting place for developing a healthy, positive self-image.

God's character and you

A key factor in understanding what is true of us as individuals in Christ is first to understand who God is. We see this in the following list of God's characteristics and what they mean to us.[2]

God is King of the universe (Ps 24:8; 1 Chron 29:11–12; 2 Chron 20:6). This means that all circumstances are ultimately in His hand. He is in control of my life.

God is righteous (Ps 119:137). He cannot sin against me.

God is just (Deut 32:4). He will always be fair with me.

God is love (1 Jn 4:8). He wants to help me get the most out of life.

God is eternal (Deut 33:27). The plan He is working out for me is everlasting.

God is all-knowing (2 Chron 16:9; Ps 139:1–6). He knows all about me and my situation and how to work it out for good.

God is everywhere (Ps 139:7–10). There is nowhere I can go that He won't take care of me.

God is all-powerful (Job 42:2). There is nothing He can't do on my behalf.

God is truth (Ps 31:5). He cannot lie to me.

God is unchangeable (Mal 3:6). I can depend on Him.
God is faithful (Rom 15:5; Ex 34:6). I can trust Him to do
   what He promises.
God is holy (Rev 15). He will be holy in all His acts.

Seeing yourself as God sees you

With this background of who God is, let's look now at who
you are, as a believer, starting at the moment you receive
Christ into your life. When you place your trust in Christ as
Saviour and Lord, the Holy Spirit baptizes (or, totally iden-
tifies) you with Christ. 'For we were all baptized by one
Spirit into one body—whether Jews or Greeks, slave or
free—and we were all given the one Spirit to drink.'[3] This
happens to you and to all Christians at the moment of salvation, giving us all a new identity.
'new creature in Christ' is found in the book of Ephesians
(ch. 1 and 2). These passages show your true position in
Christ. The theological term for this concept is *positional
truth.*

   To see ourselves as God sees us, as we really are, we must
understand our position in Christ. This proper view of
ourselves in Christ is important in developing a healthy
self-image.

   These truths about us found in Ephesians 1 are:

   We are blessed with every spiritual blessing in the heavenly
      places (v.3)
   We are chosen before the foundation of the world that we
      should be holy and blameless before Him (v.4)
   We are predestined to adoption as sons (v.5)
   We are redeemed through His blood (v.7)
   We are sealed in Him with the Holy Spirit (v.13)

Because of our position in Christ, great things are true of
us, truths that Paul wants us to know. He therefore prays

that the eyes of our heart may be enlightened, so we may know what is the hope of His calling, what are the riches of the glory of His inheritance in the saints, and what is the surpassing greatness of His power towards us who believe (vv. 18–19). God is concerned that we see ourselves as He sees us.

Paul goes on to describe Christ's resurrection and seating at the right hand of God (vv. 20–23) and says that we are also resurrected and seated with Him (Eph 2:6).

To the positional truths of Ephesians 1, we can add further descriptions of believers after they trust Christ (Eph 2:4–10). Christians are described as:

—alive together with Christ
—raised up with Christ
—seated with Him in the heavenly places
—in Christ Jesus
—saved by grace
—His workmanship

To appreciate even more what it means to be in Christ, compare the above with the following description of persons before they trust Christ (Eph 2:1–3). They are:

—dead in trespasses and sins
—walking according to the prince of the power of this world
—walking according to the prince of the power of the air
—walking according to the spirit that is now working in the sons of disobedience
—living in the lusts of the flesh and of the mind
—by nature children of wrath

If you are a believer, however, you can say the following about yourself:

I have peace with God (Rom 5:1)
I am accepted by God (Eph 1)

I am a child of God (Jn 1:12)
I am indwelt by the Holy Spirit (1 Cor 3:16)
I have access to God's wisdom (Jas 1:5)
I am helped by God (Heb 4:16)
I am reconciled to God (Rom 5:11)
I have no condemnation (Rom 8:1)
I am justified (Rom 5:1)
I have His righteousness (2 Cor 5:21; Rom 5:19)
I am His representative (2 Cor 5:20)
I am completely forgiven (Col 1:14)
I have my needs met by God (Phil 4:19)
I am tenderly loved (Jer 31:1)
I am the aroma of Christ to God (2 Cor 2:15)
I am a temple of God (1 Cor 3:16)
I am blameless and beyond reproach (Col 1:22)

Are you beginning to understand from the above what Paul meant when he emphasized, 'Therefore, if anyone is in Christ, he is a new creation; the old has gone, the new has come!'?

One of the keys to maturity is to acknowledge that at the moment of trusting Christ you 'put on the new self, which is being renewed in knowledge in the image of its Creator' (Col 3:10). You might say that as a result of being 'in Christ' we have been 're-created'.

In the following chapters you will discover more things that are spiritually true of you, as well as learn how they can become real in your daily life and relationships.

Building
a better self-image

9

Being able to remember who God is and who you are in His sight is important as you meet the traumas and stresses of life. This chapter's list of characteristics of God and of you will help you from getting 'spiritual vertigo' during tough times.

Choose some of the characteristics given in this chapter about God and you that you would like to learn by heart. Write these on record cards to carry with you as you begin to reprogramme your mind with these great truths.

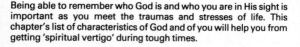

10

A New Sense of Belonging

Your personal experience with Christ is meant to provide a solid foundation for each of the three pillars of your self-image. Your sense of belonging rests on God the Father, your sense of worthiness on God the Son, and your sense of competence on God the Spirit. As you come to understand what that means and begin to experience its reality, each of those pillars will be restructured, providing support on which a stable self-image can rest.

Your most basic need is the need to be loved and to sense that you belong. You may know intellectually that you are loved, but have you ever felt loved? You may feel unlovable. Emotionally, many people claim to have a feeling of emptiness directly attributable to not feeling loved as a child. They can even describe an 'empty ache' deep in their chests, which is closely tied to their poor sense of belonging.

Unconditional love

The most significant aspect of God's thoughts and feelings about you is His unconditional love and acceptance. 'This is love: not that we loved God, but that he loved us and sent his Son as an atoning sacrifice for our sins.'[1] Nothing about you caused God to love you; He just did!

Too often people forget this basic truth that God loves

them. Before a person ever comes to Christ, He loved them and He loves them now (Rom 5:8; 8:38–39). Jesus pointed out the extent of this love when He said, 'As the Father has loved me, so have I loved you. Now remain in my love.'[2] It's staggering to think that Christ loves us as much as God the Father loves Him. In the world we live in, that's difficult to grasp intellectually, let alone experience emotionally.

When Christ was facing the cross, He prayed for His followers—those then and us now—and asked the Father to protect all of us:

> I pray for them . . . for they are yours. All I have is yours, and all you have is mine. And glory has come to me through them. I will remain in the world no longer, but they are still in the world . . . I have given them the glory that you gave me, that they may be one as we are one: I in them and you in me. May they be brought to complete unity to let the world know that you sent me and have loved them even as you have loved me.[3]

Jesus emphasized here that the Father loves you, a believer in Him, just as much as He loves the Son.

Bill and Gloria Gaither have tried to capture the depth of God's love in their song, 'I am Loved'. The first verse declares: 'I said if you knew, you wouldn't want me, my scars are hidden by the face I wear; He said, my child, my scars go deeper, it was love for you that put them there.'

The chorus relates the believer's response when grasping the extent of His love. 'I am loved, I am loved, I can risk loving you, for the One who knows me best, loves me most. I am loved, you are loved, won't you please take my hand. We are free to love each other, we are loved.'

God, the One who knows you best (Ps 139:1–6), loves you most!

Understanding this could solve the problem of Jodi Foster's actress friend, whose self-image and self-worth were so poor. She thought that if God really knew her and still loved her, He would have to be 'a fool'. If only she could realize that God knows her even better than she knows herself and still loves her so much that He sent His Son to die for her.

For most people today, it's extremely difficult to grasp such unconditional and knowledgeable love. It is a love undeserved and unmotivated. God demonstrated it by sending His Son to die for us. 'For God so loved the world that he gave his one and only Son, that whoever believes in him shall not perish but have eternal life.'⁴ God loves you and therefore, in His sight, you are lovable. 'But God demonstrates his own love for us in this: While we were still sinners, Christ died for us.'⁵

> *The One who knows you best*
> *loves you most!*

One might argue, 'Well, that love is past tense. What about right now?' Jesus also said this in the present tense, for 'the Father himself loves you.'⁶

What about the future? Is His love great enough to survive the difficulties, disappointments and frustrations that are bound to come along? To that question, too, the Bible has an answer: 'For I [Paul] am convinced that neither death nor life, neither angels nor demons, neither the present nor the future, nor any powers, neither height nor depth, nor anything else in all creation, will be able to separate us from the love of God that is in Christ Jesus our Lord.'⁷

For some of us it's difficult not only to respond to God's unconditional love, but also to the love of others. Take Rick's experience, for instance. He was visiting a friend's home when the friend felt compelled to go over to him, put his hand on Rick's shoulder and say simply, 'You know,

Rick, it's been a while since I told you "I love you."'
Immediately Rick swung round and blurted, 'What do
you want?' His friend, perplexed, responded, 'Nothing.
What are you talking about?' Rick didn't reply. Later, Rick
returned to his friend's home and asked forgiveness for the
way he had responded to that expression of love. 'I'm not
used to someone loving me when they don't want anything,'
he explained.

So often our experiences in earthly relationships become
a barrier to responding to our heavenly Father just as, in
the above true account, Rick had trouble responding to his
friend. God pointed out our problem of failing to respond
to Him by saying, 'You thought...I was just like you....'[8]

Unconditional acceptance

Other people want to argue like this with God. 'But I need
to help others first,' or 'I need to straighten out my life
before I can be accepted by You and before I can accept
myself.'

God responds, 'I already accept you. Because my Son
died for your sins, I can accept you.'

Not only does God love us unconditionally, He also
accepts us just the way we are. There is no evidence in the
Scriptures that we must *perform* to be acceptable to God.
'For it is by grace you have been saved, through faith—and
this not from yourselves, it is the gift of God—not by
works, so that no-one can boast.'[9] Our acceptance with
God is not based on our good deeds or good attitudes or on
what we have done for Him; it is a gift from Him. Our
acceptance is based on who He is and what He has done. It
becomes personal for us when we place our trust in Christ
and accept Him as Saviour and Lord. We are told that 'all
who received him, to those who believed in his name, he
gave the right to become children of God.'[10]

God is always expecting the best of us, that we will

succeed. Yet when we fail, we always have another chance with Him. He doesn't lecture us. In His grace, He never says, 'I told you so!' He allows the consequences of our sins to teach us as He applies loving discipline and chastisement. He accepts our abilities and talents and works with us and through us. In the Scriptures He presents His ideals for our lives, yet He knows that we will fall short of these time and time again.

A famous story from the annals of the Rose Bowl illustrates what it means to have someone believe in you and accept you unconditionally. (The Rose Bowl is the post-season competition between the two best college teams at American football, held in the Rose Bowl stadium in Los Angeles.)

In 1929, a University of California football player, Roy Riegels, made Rose Bowl history. In the second quarter-part of the game, he grabbed a Georgia Tech fumble and headed for the goal area, but the wrong goal area. For a moment the other players froze. Then Benny Lom, a teammate of Roy's, started after him. After making a spectacular 65-yard fumble return, a confused Riegels was downed by his own teammate, just before he scored for his opponents.

Riegels's team had to punt with their backs at their own goal line. Georgia Tech blocked the kick, made from the goal area, and earned a two-point safety margin, which eventually won them the game.

At half-time, the California players filed glumly to their dressing room. Spectators and players alike were wondering what Riegels's fate would be in the hands of California's Coach Price. In the dressing room Riegels slumped in a corner, put his face in his hands and cried uncontrollably. Coach Price was silent and offered no half-time pep talk. What could he say? As they got ready to go out for the second half, his only comment was, 'Men, the same team that played the first half will start the second.'

The players started for the door, all but Riegels. Coach

Price walked to the corner where Riegels sat and said quietly, 'Roy, didn't you hear me? I said, "The same team that played the first half will start the second."' Roy replied, 'Coach, I can't do it. I've ruined you, the University of California and myself. I couldn't face that crowd in the stadium to save my life.' Coach Price put his hand on his player's shoulder and said, 'Roy, get up and go back; the game is only half over.' So Roy Riegels went out to play again—harder, said the Georgia Tech players afterwards, than they had ever seen anyone play before.

When Dr J. Haddon Robinson told this story in *Campus Life* magazine, he went on to say, 'When I think of this story, I think, "What a coach!"'

'And then I think about all the big mistakes I've made in life and how God is willing to forgive me and let me try again. I take the ball and run in the wrong direction. I stumble and fall and am so ashamed of myself that I never want to show my face again. But God comes to me and bends over me in the person of His Son Jesus Christ, and he says, "Get up and go on back; the game is only half over."

'That's the gospel of the second chance. Of the third chance. Of the hundredth chance.

'And when I think of that, I have to say, "What a God!"'[11]

Accepting ourselves

If you are already a Christian, think for a moment about what happened to you when you trusted Christ as your Saviour and were accepted by God as His child. You were born again (Jn 3:3–5; 1 Pet 1:23) as a child of God (Jn 1:12–13). You became an heir of God (Eph 1:13–14; Rom 8:17) and were adopted into God's family (Eph 1:5). You were loved by God the Father (Rom 5:8; 1 Jn 4:9–10) who poured His love into your heart (Rom 5:5). You became one with Christ in such a way that you will never be parted from Him (Jn 17:23; Gal 2:20; Heb 13:5); nothing will ever separate you from God's love (Rom 8:38-39). You are going to spend eternity with the One who loves you in His house (Jn 14:1-4). You entered a new family to which you now belong (1 Cor 12:13, 17).

When we realize that God already accepts us, we next begin to look at ourselves, asking, 'Then can I accept myself?'

The fact that God accepts us should be our motivation for accepting ourselves. If we cannot accept ourselves the way we are, with our limitations and assets, weaknesses as well as strengths, shortcomings as well as abilities, then we cannot trust anyone else to accept us the way we are. We will always be putting on a front, building a façade around ourselves, never letting people know what we are really like deep down inside.

Once you see that God accepts you, it is easier to accept yourself unconditionally. Then you can more easily trust other people to accept you, and you can unconditionally accept others the way they are too.

One of the greatest needs in the church today is for Christians to live out the scriptural admonition: 'Accept one another . . . just as Christ accepted you, in order to bring praise to God.'[12]

Belonging to the family

I belong! I'm a child of God and I belong to His family. The apostle John made an acute observation when, under the Spirit's guidance, he wrote, 'How great is the love the Father has lavished on us, that we should be called children of God! And that is what we are!' Right after saying we are 'called children of God', John must have paused and realized what God had just shown him, for he followed that important truth with the exclamation, 'And that is what we are!'[13]

There comes a time in the lives of all of us when we ought to pause and say, And that is what I am—a child of God—

and realize what that means.

We are God's children, adopted into His family. Some of us, however, may think that adopted children hold lesser positions in a family than do naturally born children. I am impressed with how one father, Dick Day, dean of the Julian Center (a three-month intensive discipleship pro-gramme), has dispelled that notion. After having five children of their own, he and his wife Charlotte went to Korea and adopted Jimmy, a five-year-old orphan.

'That little fellow, Jimmy,' Dick now says, 'is my son. He has the same privileges and rights as our five other children, the same rights to our inheritance, our time and our love.'

Dick's statement raised my level of appreciation for the place we hold in the family of God, as adopted children and co-heirs with Christ, God's only begotten Son.

No longer an island

Jesus said, 'Believe me when I say that I am in the Father and the Father is in me.'[14] Two people are in that union, God the Father and God the Son. The next few verses talk about God's sending a third Person, the Holy Spirit. And then Christ said, 'On that day [which refers to Pentecost and the establishment of the body of Christ], you will realise that I am in my Father, and you are in me, and I am in you.'[15]

Do you see what that passage means, 'I am in the Father and you in me and I in you'?

It says that when you confess Christ as Saviour and Lord, you are in the Father and the Father is in you. What's more, you are in Christ and Christ is in you.

Now, follow closely. I'm in the Father. The Father is in us. And so you are in me and I'm in you. As a Christian, I'm not an island, I'm a peninsula. I'm a part of the body of Christ; I belong to the body of Christ. I'm one of the vital, living members talked about in 1 Corinthians 12:

For we were all baptised by one Spirit into one body...and we were all given the one Spirit to drink.... But God has combined the members of the body and has given greater honour to the parts that lacked it, so that there should be no division in the body, but that its parts should have equal concern for each other. If one part suffers, every part suffers with it; if one part is honoured, every part rejoices with it. Now you are the body of Christ, and each one of you is a part of it.'[16]

Understanding that we belong to God the Father and His family, that we are unconditionally accepted and loved by Him, is the key to restructuring our sense of belonging.

Building a better self-image

10

List five people whom you believe love you; list one way each person has demonstrated love for you.

_____

_____

_____

_____

_____

What would God have to do to prove to you that He loves you?

_____

_____

(See Rom 5:8; 1 Jn 4:9–10.) _____

What is the greatest act of love a person can give? (Read John 15:13.) _____

Do you love anyone that much? _____ Who loves you that much? _____ God loves you that much.

In your own words, state what God did to show His great love for you. _____

_____

11

A New Sense of Worthiness

Even though we know that Christ died for our sins and made us worthy, sometimes it's easy to feel that He didn't die for us personally. He just died for the whole world or for other people, and we were able to be included in what was meant for them.

Yet if you had been the only person alive, Christ still would have died for you. You may have heard that before, but did you believe it? Think it through. If you were the only person alive, then you would stand in the place of Adam. Just as Adam did, you would have sinned. And as He did for Adam, God would have provided a redeemer (Gen 3:15), this time just for you.

Worth forgiving

Can you believe then that God continues to forgive you, daily, for the sins you commit? In living the Christian life, we fail every day. Yet every day God forgives us. We're told, 'If we confess our sins, he is faithful and just and will forgive us our sins and purify us from all unrighteousness.'[1]

In Hebrews 10:12 we read, 'This priest [Jesus] had offered for all time one sacrifice for sins.' The effects of this once-and-for-all sacrifice are seen in Colossians, 'He forgave us all our sins, having cancelled the written code, with its regulations, that was against us and that stood opposed to us.[2] For God it was a costly forgiveness. 'For you know that it was not with perishable things such as silver or gold that you were redeemed from the empty way of life handed down to you from your forefathers, but with the precious blood of Christ.'[3]

Listen to King David confessing his sins to God: 'Then I acknowledged my sin to you and did not cover up my iniquity. I said, "I will confess my transgressions to the Lord"—and you forgave the guilt of my sin.'[4] What freedom, to know we're forgiven by God! 'Therefore, there is now no condemnation for those who are in Christ Jesus.'[5]

On the other hand, some people are sure that God could never forgive them because they have sinned too much, too long, or too greatly. A seventeen-year-old student wrote to me, saying:

> The reason I'm writing this is because I'm alone and confused. . . . I had sex with my boyfriend, thinking I owed it to him. About four months later I learned I was pregnant. . . . I had an abortion. . . . Jeff left me, and my parents still don't know. About a month ago I became a Christian. . . . I have been feeling guilty. How can God love me after all I have done? I just don't feel that my life is worth living any more. . . . I cry myself to sleep every night. I just wish sometimes I were dead. My parents and I don't get along too well. They have been Christians all their life and they wouldn't understand what I am going through. . . . I'm just so confused. Can God really love and forgive me? Please write back.

That young woman doesn't realize the significance of Christ's death on the cross and how it relates to her. If only she could grasp the good news of forgiveness. The good news, the gospel, is that if we confess our sins—the ones we are aware of—then God freely forgives us 'all sins'.

A good illustration of 'all sins' is the life of King Manasseh, one of Judah's most wicked kings. He turned his back on

God, worshipped false gods and led the people in idolatry (2 Chron 33:1–9). If the young writer of the above letter believed that God would not forgive her, then, without hesitation, she would have to say that God would not forgive Manasseh.

History, however, shows that the Assyrians captured Manasseh, and while captive he humbled himself before God. Despite Manasseh's evil past, God lovingly and compassionately forgave him. If every person could grasp how completely and extensively God forgives, there would be so much more joy in the world.

> He does not treat us as our sins deserve or repay us according to our iniquities. For as high as the heavens are above the earth, so great is his love for those who fear him; as far as the east is from the west, so far has he removed our transgressions from us. As a father has compassion on his children, so the Lord has compassion on those who fear him.[6]

Forgiving ourselves

Another exciting aspect about God's forgiveness is that if He forgives us, we can forgive ourselves. Too often Christians come to the place where they can accept God's forgiveness but still can't forgive themselves. Isn't it interesting that we can be harder on ourselves than God is? We demand more of ourselves and put more conditions on ourselves for forgiveness than our heavenly Father does.

If Christ died for our sins and God forgives us, then why can't we forgive ourselves? To have a healthy self-image, we desperately need to see ourselves as God sees us—forgiven.

Some time ago I said something in a restaurant that I never should have said. It hurt a brother in Christ deeply. On the way home I realized the impact of my uncalled for, off-the-cuff remark. I returned to the restaurant, trying to find the one I had hurt so deeply.

Whose forgiveness?

I acknowledged to this Christian brother that what I had done was a sin and asked for his forgiveness. He looked me squarely in the eye and said, 'I won't forgive you. Someone in your position should never have said that.' Not quite knowing what to do, I responded, 'I know I never should have said it; that's why I'm asking your forgiveness.' I did all I could to make it right, but that man wouldn't budge in his determination not to forgive me.

I went home frustrated and confused. I began to struggle spiritually and emotionally over the situation. Feeling extremely guilty, I began to berate myself verbally. 'How could you have said that?' I asked myself accusingly. 'How can you be in Christian work and hurt a brother like that? How can God use you when you act like that?'

My unceasing self-chastisement must have sounded as if I were writing a new hymn titled 'Oh, Woe Is Me', about self-pity and the misery of personal guilt. Then God the Holy Spirit began to work in my thinking. I stopped and thought through the entire incident, including my subsequent response to it, in the light of Scripture and my relationship with Christ. Mentally I said, 'Just a moment, Josh, you're not handling this right. You can make one of two responses to this situation. One, you can continue to feel sorry for yourself, wallow around in guilt, question God's ability to deal with the situation and to use you, and look at your own frailty and sin. Two, you can realize that Jesus died for this situation, do all you can to make it right with your brother, confess it to God, accept His forgiveness and recognize His ability to handle the situation. Then recognizing His righteousness, forgive yourself, lift up your head, put your shoulders back and your eyes on Christ, and go forward walking by faith.'

After wrestling a short while with the alternatives, I chose to acknowledge God's forgiveness, forgive myself, continue to walk by faith and do all I could from then on to heal the relationship with a wounded, unforgiving brother.

At that point there was an awareness that accepting God's forgiveness and subsequently forgiving myself was not dependent on or conditioned by the other person's forgiving me, even though God did expect me to do all I could to make it right. 'Therefore, if you are offering your gift at the altar and there remember that your brother has something against you, leave your gift there in front of the altar. First go and be reconciled to your brother; then come and offer your gift.'[7]

A year later, reminiscing about the incident, I remarked to my wife, 'Dear, I think that relationship has healed. The hurt seems to be gone and, from all appearances, I think he's forgiven me. In fact, I think the relationship is better than it was before.'

As we realize that God forgives us, why do we refuse to forgive ourselves? In fact, what right do we have not to forgive ourselves? He is the One with the right to say you're forgiven and worthy—not you and your feelings.

And God not only forgives you. He says, 'Their sins and lawless acts I will remember no more.'[8] If you have 'the mind of Christ,'[9] then you too must forgive—not condemn —yourself, and be willing to forget even yesterday's sins.

Giving forgiveness

The beautiful thing about developing a healthy self-image in the area of forgiveness is that you're able not only to forgive yourself, but you're able to be a channel or instrument in forgiving others. 'Be kind and compassionate to one another, forgiving each other, just as in Christ God forgave you.'[10]

Experiencing forgiveness is one of the greatest needs in the world today. A director of a mental hospital said in a university seminar that half of his patients could go home if they could know they were forgiven.

One way God communicates forgiveness is through His children. Another verse in the Gaither song 'I Am Loved' clearly describes this: 'Forgiven, I repeat, I am forgiven, clean before my Lord I freely stand. Forgiven, I can dare forgive my brother, forgiven, I can reach out to take your hand.'

> *Experiencing forgiveness is*
> *one of the greatest needs in*
> *the world today.*

As fallen sinners, our efforts in producing a righteous standing with God are worthless (Is 64:6) but, as objects of His creation, we are not worthless. His creation of us, combined with His love for us, and demonstrated by His work in us, makes us of significant value. Yet, remember, it is not because of what we have done but because of who He is and what He has done.

Worthy, yet fallen

If we define a healthy self-image as 'seeing yourself as God sees you—no more, no less,' then we must see not only humanity's worth in the eyes of God, but also humanity's sinfulness, rebellion and alienation from God.

The Bible is clear about human fallenness and depravity. God personally remarked that the human heart is 'deceitful above all things, and desperately wicked.'[11]

Anyone who wants a balanced picture of human nature would need to consider God's perspective as it is related in Psalm 53:2–3: 'God looks down from heaven on the sons of men to see if there are any who understand, any who seek God. Everyone has turned away, they have together become corrupt; there is no-one who does good, not even one.'

Human sinfulness is universal, 'All have sinned and fall short of the glory of God.'[12] Some of us don't want to admit this reality, particularly about ourselves. However, 'if we say we have no sin, we deceive ourselves, and the truth is not in us.'[13]

In the Old Testament we're told that the Hebrew warriors used slingshots as weapons. Some of the warriors were extremely accurate in their aim. They could 'sling a stone at a hair and not miss.'[14] The word translated 'miss' is *chatah*, which basically means 'to miss the mark'. In other places in the Old Testament the word *chatah* is translated 'to sin'.

The New Testament has this same concept of sin. Paul used a similar analogy of sinning when he used the Greek word *hamartano*. Sinning is missing the mark, the standard, the objective for our lives that God set up for us when He created us. This is the word used in Romans 3:23. It means to fall short of the holy, just, righteous nature of God.

Self-image and God's image

Although we all are deeply infected by sin, this falling away from or missing the mark of what God intended for us has not entirely destroyed our Godlikeness. Because of sin, humanity does not become less than human. There is still a huge gap between all other created beings and human beings. In the creation God did something that laid a permanent basis for human dignity and worth. God made us a special creation when He said, 'Let us make man in our image, in our likeness.'[15]

This 'image of God' has been marred by humanity's fall into sin, but it has not been destroyed. Paul referred even to the Corinthians, who were living in active sin, as still bearing 'the image and glory of God.'[16]

If you diminish the fact that you bear the image of God, you may have been thinking of yourself as no better than a tree. Granted, both are living creations of God, yet there is a crucial difference. Your creation in the image of God gives you intellectual abilities, emotions, the ability to make decisions about right and wrong, the power of creativity and the capacity to love and communicate.

The exact nature of what constitutes this 'image of God' in humankind isn't certain. We know, however, that it still exists in humanity even after the Fall into sin. It is the basis for the sacredness and value of human life (Gen 9:6).

Francis Schaeffer writes, 'It is important to note that fallen man still retains something of the image of God. The Fall separates man from God, but it does not remove his original differentiation from other things. Fallen man is not less than man.'

In order to emphasize our individual value even after the Fall, Jesus made a comparison between the worthiness of humanity and all the birds that God cares for. 'Look at the birds of the air; they do not sow or reap or store away in barns, and yet your heavenly Father feeds them. Are you not much more valuable then they?... So don't be afraid; you are worth more than many sparrows.'[17]

Jesus also showed that humanity was worth more than other animals when, in answer to antagonists who thought He should not heal on the Sabbath, He said, 'If any of you has a sheep and it falls into a pit on the Sabbath, will you not take hold of it and lift it out? How much more valuable is a man than a sheep!'[18]

Many writers have quoted Martin Luther's words: 'God does not love us because we are valuable; we are valuable because God loves us.' The statement is true, but perhaps it doesn't go far enough. As is, it easily could be misleading. To the statement, 'We are valuable because God loves us' let's add the words, 'and has expressed His love by creating us in His image and, then, *re-creating* us in Christ.'

Greater worth

Re-creating us in Christ gives us something as good as, if not better than, that original unflawed image of God. 'For God took the sinless Christ and *poured into him our sins*. Then, in exchange, *He poured God's goodness into us*!'[19] (Italics mine).

If you consider how good God's goodness or righteousness really is, it becomes awesome to realize that you have this goodness right now. Not only are you worthy because you were created worthy, but you have a greater worthiness because of the Cross of Christ and His love for you. You are worthy because of your creation and your redemption.

Several centuries ago a great scholar, Morena, was forced to live as a Protestant exile. Falling seriously ill in Lombardy, Italy, he was taken to a paupers' hospital. The doctors, assuming the wretched-looking man could not speak Latin, began speaking that language among themselves at his bedside. They said, 'This one is going to die anyway, so let's try an experiment on this worthless creature.' On hearing that, Dr Morena raised up, looked at the physicians and said, 'What Jesus died for, how can you call worthless?'

Understanding what Jesus did for you can restructure your pillar of worthiness, your sense of self-worth, and give added stability to your image of who you are.

Building a better self-image

II

1 John 1:9 states, 'If we confess our sins, he is faithful and just and will forgive us our sins and purify us from all unrighteousness.' The word *confess* means to agree with God concerning your sin. It simply means acknowledging that you have sinned and that Jesus died for that sin too.

What sin or sins do you acknowledge to God right now?

_____

_____

_____

What does 1 John 1:9 say God is doing about your sins?

_____

From how much unrighteousness does God cleanse you?

_____

_____

What does God say He will do once you have confessed your sins? (Read Heb 9:22.) _____

How far away from you have your sins been removed? (Read Ps 103:12.) _____

_____

How pure and clean does the Lord make you? (Read Is 1:18.)

_____

Read 2 Corinthians 5:21. Who took your sins? _____

Whose righteousness did you receive? _____

12

A New Sense of Competence

Now let's look at that third pillar, competence, which so
many people have had knocked loose in the harsh experiences of ordinary life. For you, it may have begun with an
unreconciled dependence on your mother or father to take
care of all your needs, which did not allow you to develop
self-confidence. Or maybe you have faced failure after
failure through the years. Or perhaps just one devastating
blow, like divorce or the loss of your job, damaged or
destroyed your sense of competence.

Whatever the cause, without a sense of competence we
lose courage and hope and become pessimistic about life
in general. We each need that inner sense of confidence
that says, 'I can do it!'

Competence through the Spirit

No matter why your pillar of competence is weak or non-
existent, it still can be rebuilt and transformed. As you
come to understand and experience your relationship with
God the Holy Spirit, your confidence can be restored.

The Bible has a lot to say about our relationship to the
Holy Spirit, things of which many Christians are unaware.
We have been born of the Spirit (Jn 3:3–5). The Spirit lives
within us (Jn 14:7) and will be with us for ever (Jn 14:16).

The Spirit teaches us what we need to know (Jn 14:26) and testifies to us that we *belong,* that we are God's children (Rom 8:16). He guides us (Rom 8:14) and provides for us the talents, abilities and spiritual gifts that we need to live purposeful lives serving God (1 Cor 12:4, 11). The Spirit helps us in our weakness and intercedes for us (Rom 8:26–27). He is the one who develops in us the fruit of God's righteousness: love, joy, peace, patience, kindness, goodness, faithfulness, gentleness and self-control (Gal 5:22–23).

The most effective way to grasp the potential competence you have through the Holy Spirit is to understand the resources available to every Christian as a result of the Spirit's indwelling presence.

Something wonderful happened to the Lord's disciples on the day of Pentecost. They were filled with the Holy Spirit and went forth in His power to change the course of history. That same Holy Spirit who empowered the disciples to live holy lives and to be powerful and fruitful witnesses wants to work in us today. The amazing fact that Jesus Christ lives in us and expresses His love through us is one of the most important truths in the Word of God.

The impossible life

Trying to live the impossible standards of the Christian life in our own strength—and failing, as we inevitably do—is bound to weaken our sense of competence. In fact, the Christian who tries to be as much like Christ as possible (a supernatural ideal) can have a worse sense of competence than the person who is not a Christian and who chooses to live by some human ideal. The standards of the Christian life are too high for us to achieve on our own. According to the Word of God, only one person has been able to succeed in keeping them—Jesus Christ. The Christian life was meant to be lived only in the power of His Holy Spirit.

Not only does the Holy Spirit enable the Christian to be

born into God's family, but the Spirit assists the Christian in spiritual growth, in producing the fruit of the Spirit.

It is the Holy Spirit who empowers us to be fruitful witnesses. When Jesus said that we were to be his 'witnesses both in Jerusalem, and in all Judea and Samaria, and even to the remotest part of the earth, ' He preceded this with the statement that 'You shall receive power when the Holy Spirit has come upon you.'[1] It's not only impossible to become a Christian apart from the Holy Spirit, it's also impossible to produce the fruit of the Spirit in our lives and to introduce others to Jesus.

From the point that we receive Christ and are indwelt by the Spirit, everything we need to be men and women of God and to be fruitful for Christ is available to us. The key lies in allowing the Holy Spirit to fill or empower our lives, so we can experience all that is available to us. It's important to realize that the word for *fill* does not mean something from outside coming in but rather something already inside doing the filling. That is why I prefer using the words *permeate* or *empower*.

We are filled with the Spirit by faith, faith in an all-powerful God who loves us. When you take a cheque to the bank and you know you have money there, you don't go in with doubts about whether or not the bank will cash your cheque. You don't expect to have to beg the cashier to give you the money. Instead, you simply go 'in faith', place the cheque on the counter and expect to receive the money that is already yours. In asking God to fill us completely with the Holy Spirit who is already in our lives, we again simply ask for something that is already ours as children of God.

While you can expect to receive both your money from the bank and the filling of the Holy Spirit from God by faith alone, nevertheless you must recognize the factors that precede receiving both of these. You receive your money from the bank only when you go there with a cheque that is properly filled in and signed. If you go there brashly, without following the bank's procedures for disbursing funds, it's not likely that you will receive your money. Merely standing on the kerb outside the bank and yelling, 'I want my money!' won't get the desired results.

Similarly, several things prepare you for the filling of the Holy Spirit. First, you must hunger and thirst for God and sincerely desire to be filled with His Spirit. Jesus' promise was 'Blessed are those who hunger and thirst for righteousness, for they shall be satisfied.'[2]

Second, you must be willing to surrender the direction and control of your life to Christ. As Paul said, 'And so, dear brothers, I plead with you to give your bodies to God. Let them be a living sacrifice, holy—the kind he can accept. When you think of what he has done for you, is this too much to ask'[3]

Third, confess every known sin the Holy Spirit brings to your mind and accept the cleansing and forgiveness that God promises. 'But if we confess our sins to him, he can be depended upon to forgive us and to cleanse us from every wrong. And it is perfectly proper for God to do this for us because Christ died to wash away our sins.'[4]

Filled—to be or not to be

Being filled with the Spirit is not an optional lifestyle for the Christian. God commands us to be filled with His Spirit. 'Do not get drunk on wine, which leads to debauchery. Instead, be filled with the Spirit.'[5] But God does not command without providing us with a way to obey His commands. He gives us the promise 'that if we ask anything according to his will, he hears us. And if we know that he hears us—whatever we ask—we know that we have what we asked of him.'[6]

Christians already have the Holy Spirit dwelling within them, so they need not ask Him to come into their lives. They need only ask Him to fill and take control of every part, every hidden corner and crevice.

While Christians are *indwelt* only once by the Spirit (at the time Christ came into our lives through the Holy Spirit), we will be *filled with* the Spirit many times. In fact, the Greek wording means 'be ye being filled,' referring to a constant and continual filling of the Spirit to control and empower one's life.

The frustration of self-effort is eliminated when we live in the power of the Holy Spirit. He alone can give us the ability to live the holy and meaningful life we so desire.

If you know that you desire a life filled with the Spirit, you need only to ask the Father for it. Acknowledge that you have been in control of your life, which is sin against God, the rightful ruler of your life. Thank Him for forgiving your sins through Christ's death on the Cross for you. Invite Christ to take over the control of your life and ask the Holy Spirit to fill you with His power so that you can glorify Christ in all you do.

As an act of faith, then thank Him for doing what you have asked. Thanking Him is no presumption, it is acting in faith that He is keeping His promises to give us whatever we ask within His will. And since He commands us to be filled with His Spirit, it is His will for all Christians to live this supernatural lifestyle.

From the sense of competence that his experience with the Holy Spirit gave Paul, he could say, 'I can do everything through him who gives me strength.'[7] Paul saw his adequacy not in himself but in God, whom He had come to know as an integral part of His life. 'Not that we are competent to claim anything for ourselves but our competence comes from God.'[8]

Weaknesses into strengths

In studying the people whom God uses, you often find that when they yield themselves to God, He takes their limitations and turns them into strengths.

So often people say, 'Oh, John or Mary ought to be in a special kind of Christian work. He or she is so talented, so persuasive, so gifted in that particular area.' But sometimes strengths can end up being limitations. The strengths we relied on, before God had complete control of our life, can sometimes become disadvantages. We tend to lean on whatever strengths were evident in us before we consciously allowed the Holy Spirit to build other strengths into our life. The strengths we had before the Holy Spirit took control are sometimes temptations for attitudes of self-sufficiency, self-centredness and pride.

On the other hand, weaknesses we were aware of and knew we would have to rely on God to overcome can keep us dependent on the Holy Spirit to change. These may turn into some of our greatest strengths.

The strong and the weak

A proper perspective of yourself is understanding who you are with your strengths and good points, your shortcomings and faults, remembering that those surface strengths can become temptations for pride. Having a healthy self-image doesn't mean you don't have limitations. If you know who you are in Christ, you are free to accept your weaknesses, faults and mistakes—and not be threatened by them. Patiently and with hope, you can work through those problems without putting yourself down because you don't meet some imagined standard of perfection.

Someone with a sturdy pillar of competence can affirm the axiom mentioned earlier: 'I'm not what I ought (or was created) to be, but I'm not what I used to be and, by God's grace, I'm not what I'm going to be.' We can be 'confident of this, that he who began a good work in [us] will carry it on to completion until the day of Christ Jesus.'[9]

Building a better self-image

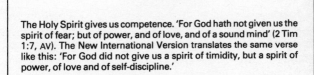

12

The Holy Spirit gives us competence. 'For God hath not given us the spirit of fear; but of power, and of love, and of a sound mind' (2 Tim 1:7, AV). The New International Version translates the same verse like this: 'For God did not give us a spirit of timidity, but a spirit of power, of love and of self-discipline.'

Which spirit given above is not from God? _____

_____. Which spirit is from God? _____

_____

Philippians 4:13 reads, 'I can do everything through him who gives me strength.' Does this mean we are potentially competent to do whatever God wants us to do?

_____

_____

_____

_____

_____

13

The Process of Re-parenting

Many Christians have reached out, taken hold of all the fullness of God as best they know how and years later are still unsatisfied with their view of themselves and their progress in the Christian life. Maybe you are one of those Christians. You may even have been used by God in wonderful ways. Perhaps you are looked up to as the epitome of faith and maturity, yet basically you still see yourself as a poor specimen of God's creation. You may never have seen that your Christian growth should include developing a better view of who you are or why you had such an unhealthy view of yourself in the first place.

God's plan for healing unhealthy self-images and personalities is patterned after his original parenting process. The original process was designed to mould healthy personalities too, but when sin entered the world the original became deeply distorted.

Previously we discovered three major elements of the parenting process. The first of these is *modelling*. Parents are to serve as examples for their children. The second element is *teaching*. Parents are to teach their children (which includes disciplining them) the practical knowledge needed to survive in the world. For Christian parents this includes giving their children a solid Christian home along with educating them in God's Word. The third element is *learning to relate.* A child's relationships with parents provide the atmosphere that makes the first two elements effective. Without quality relationships of love, understanding, and acceptance, the modelling and teachng are ineffective.

From parenting to re-parenting

A person's spiritual life also begins with birth and grows through a parenting process. Its initial step is conversion. When you accept Christ, you begin to reverse the process of sin that has passed from generation to generation and to shift the direction of your life towards spiritual and emotional health. The re-parenting process has started. Growth towards becoming like Christ has begun. This growth process is a re-parenting, as spiritual and emotional needs that were not met by relationships with your human parents are now met by God—through members of the Body of Christ.

Many people alive today have been born into grossly inadequate homes. They have grown up in an atmosphere that barely provided the minimal emotional support for physical survival. When they become Christians, they may have much further to go in becoming Christlike than a person raised in a home that more adequately provided a foundation for emotional health. Usually the more adequate the original parenting process, the less re-parenting is necessary.

A lot of the process, of course, depends on the individual's own desire and willingness to become whole. But inadequately parented people often have much more to overcome in the area of trusting a heavenly Parent. The knowledge that they ought to trust God, and even the desire for Him to mould them into His image, carries them only so far and often they don't know why.

Christian growth progresses best in an atmosphere that provides the emotional support and love that the childhood home should have provided. The Body of Christ, whether a formal church, a small group of Christian friends, or a Christian work or living situation, should establish such an atmosphere and provide the necessary ingredients for growth.

Christian growth in the early church

The programme God designed to help transform a person's self-image and personality can be seen in the early church in the book of Acts.

> They devoted themselves to the apostles' teaching and to the fellowship, to the breaking of bread and to prayer. Everyone was filled with awe, and many wonders and miraculous signs were done by the apostles. All the believers were together and had everything in common. Selling their possessions and goods, they gave to anyone as he had need.[1]

The emphasis in the New Testament church seems to have been on three experiences in which every believer is to take part.[2] The first of these is a vital teaching experience: 'They devoted themselves to the apostles' teaching.' Second is a vital relational experience: 'And to the fellowship, to the breaking of bread and to prayer... All the believers were together and had everything in common.' Third is a vital witnessing experience. Witnessing in the New Testament consisted of living the Christian life and then talking about it. It was a witnessing ministry to each other as well as to the non-Christian world around them.

> Every day they continued to meet together in the temple courts. They broke bread in their homes and ate together with glad and sincere hearts, praising God and enjoying the favour of all the people. And the Lord added to their number daily those who were being saved.[3]

Re-parenting and discipleship

The Body of Christ is to be involved in these three elements of the re-parenting process—both as a child and a parent—receiving and giving intertwinedly, not only formally but in everyday situations with one another. Through these three experiences every Christian is to progress towards maturity. This is what we often call *discipleship*. One might call it a re-parenting process.

That a parallel exists between the parenting process and the re-parenting or discipleship process is not a coincidence. In the parenting process, the physical parents are meant to be the agents of growth. In the re-parenting process, the Body of Christ—with every member serving as both a child and a parent—is meant to be an agent of growth.

The Word of God in re-parenting

To transform our lives as Christians, God uses another agent as well: the Word of God. The Holy Spirit works through the body of believers and His Word to help us become like Jesus Christ. Peter wrote to us: 'Like newborn babies, crave pure spiritual milk, so that by it you may grow up in your salvation, now that you have tasted that the Lord is good.'[4] By renewing our minds, the Holy Spirit uses the Word of God to restructure our thinking (Rom 12:2). Paul wrote:

> It was he who gave some to be apostles, some to be prophets some to be evangelists, and some to be pastors and teachers, to prepare God's people for works of service, so that the body of Christ may be built up until we all reach unity in the faith and in the knowledge of the Son of God and become mature, attaining to the whole measure of the fulness of Christ.
> Then we will no longer be infants, tossed back and forth by the waves, and blown here and there by every wind of teaching and by the cunning and craftiness of men in their deceitful

scheming. Instead, speaking the truth in love, we will in all things grow up into him who is the Head, that is, Christ.[5]

The 'one-another concepts'

Through His Word, God reveals His attributes, character and personality. Through the body of Christ, He makes them a reality. Approximately sixty times in the New Testament there appear the 'one-another concepts'. These are principles that describe the way God ministers to members of the Body of Christ through each other.

These concepts include being devoted to one another (Rom 12:10), honouring one another (also Rom 12:10), being of the same mind with one another (Rom 15:5), accepting one another (Rom 15:7), admonishing one another (Rom 15:14), greeting one another (Rom 16:3–6, 16), serving one another (Gal 5:13), carrying one another's burdens (Gal 6:2), bearing with one another in love (Eph 4:2), submitting to one another (Eph 5:21) and encouraging one another (1 Thess 5:11).

Revealing God through the Body of Christ

Jesus told His disciples when He was here on earth that He came to reveal the Father to us. He said, 'Anyone who has seen me has seen the Father.... Don't you believe that I am in the Father, and that the Father is in me? The words I say to you are not just my own. Rather, it is the Father, living in me, who is doing his work.'[6]

Jesus in His physical body revealed God to the world. He made the character and attributes of God real; he put flesh and bones to God's personality. We know what God is like because Jesus made Him known to us. Could it be that the church is to reveal God something like Jesus did? The answer is *yes*. The church is called the Body of Christ and one of its purposes is to demonstrate the character and attributes of God the Father to people living today.

A young woman was asked how God could make His love for her real. She thought for a minute and said, 'He could show it to me!' Isn't that what the Body of Christ is to do, to bring God's love into reality? It's one thing for a person to read about God's love in the Scriptures or to hear about it in a sermon. It becomes real to that person when he or she experiences God's love through members of the Body of Christ.

Perhaps you remember such an experience in your own life, or perhaps God's forgiveness became real to you when a friend expressed that he or she forgave you.

By divine design the re-parenting process through the Body of Christ parallels the parenting process. This chart helps clarify that parallel.

	Parenting	Re-parenting
GOD'S AGENTS	PARENTS	BODY OF CHRIST
Behavioural examples	Modelling	Witnessing
Vital learning experiences	Teaching	Teaching
Vital relational experiences	Relationship	Fellowship

Applying the re-parenting process

Our self-images are changed by submitting ourselves to God's divine parenting process. He has provided a means whereby you can have your self-image restructured and transformed, but you must be receptive to that process.

Pinpointing your needs. The first step you must take is to become aware of the areas of your personality that need to be transformed. What are the blocks to your personal growth? Which pillar in your self-image is the weakest? It may be the one you've paid little attention to, thinking it less important than the pillar you felt was strongest (and which, therefore, you felt was most important). Or it may be one you've considered strong previously, but which you now see as a strength built on false premises.

The best way to begin to know yourself is to pray and ask God to show you through His Word what He wants changed. Seek to find what God sees as important. Begin with the Psalmist's prayer: 'Search me, O God, and know my heart; try me and know my anxious thoughts; and see if there be any hurtful way in me, and lead me in the everlasting way.'[7]

At times you will need help with this process, in which case it may be helpful to consult a mature Christian friend, pastor or Christian counsellor.

Finding help through the Scriptures. Once you have an understanding of where you are in building your pillars and what you need to work on, begin to study the Scriptures with your need in mind. You will see things in the Scriptures meant 'just for you' that you never saw before. Specific, goal-oriented Bible study can provide much of the input needed to begin your transformation.

There is a power in the Word of God that transforms lives. When a person studies and meditates on a passage of Scripture that applies to his or her problem, dramatic results occur. Often these results can be explained only as a supernatural working of the Holy Spirit. The Spirit takes the Word of God and uses it to restructure and transform the person's self-image and personality.

Finding help through the Body. The final step in the process is to allow members of the Body of Christ to be instruments of the Holy Spirit to begin to transform you. It's interesting that all of the 'one-another' passages in the

New Testament contain a dual responsibility. For example, notice Galatians 6:2: 'Carry each other's burdens, and in this way you will fulfil the law of Christ.' Our responsibility is obvious: Christians are to help with one another's burdens. But that means people must be willing to let their burdens be shared. We are to allow others to help carry our burdens too. We are to let them love us and care for us just as we should be doing for them.

Through the Body of Christ we begin to experience God's love and attributes personally. As we relate to one another, we make His character and personality real in such a way that our lives begin to be transformed. Our relationships with others become catalysts to produce healing in our lives.

As I experience God's love through you, as I experience God's comfort, mercy and justice through you, my self-image begins to change. When you forgive me and respond to me as if I am truly worthy, in time I come to believe it myself. As you trust me, believe in me and encourage me, I come to trust myself and believe in myself. I develop a new sense of competence. My personality is transformed through my relationship with you as the Holy Spirit works in me. The Body of Christ reinforces the truths I have learned from the Word of God.

> *The Body of Christ reinforces*
> *the truths I have learned*
> *from the Word of God.*

Circle of acceptance

Growth in self-acceptance and development of a better, healthier self-image are a circular experience. It begins as you start to understand God's love and acceptance. Again, it is important to realize that your true base of acceptance or confidence is in God, not in others. As you grow in this knowledge you come to believe that you are lovable and acceptable. At this point you can develop a healthy self-acceptance.

From confidence derived from your new self-acceptance, you can relate more openly with others. You express love and acceptance of them more freely. As these relationships improve and you draw closer to one another, you get a clearer view of yourself and experience God's love and acceptance in still stronger ways.

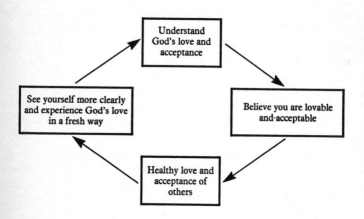

Paul's example

In 1 Thessalonians 2:1–12, Paul gave an example of the re-parenting process as he used it in his ministry. He described how he was tender with the Christians at Thessalonica, like a nursing mother (v.7). He described how he exhorted, encouraged and implored them as a father would (v.11). He emphasized his relationship with them: 'We loved you so much that we were delighted to share with you not only the gospel of God but our lives as well, because you had become so dear to us' (v.8).

There Paul's employment of a re-parenting process like the one described above is evident. He *taught* his converts. He *related* to them in love and understanding. He *modelled or witnessed* to them what it meant to be a godly person.

Note that in two places here Paul called them brothers, even though, as an apostle, he could have spoken as an authority figure. This is an important distinction to keep in mind in our relationships in the Body of Christ. In the original parenting process, there is both an authoritative component and a relational component. When we were children, our parents filled both of those roles. Now, as believers, God exercises the authoritative component and our brothers and sisters in Christ exercise the relational component. This may be what Jesus had in mind when He said, 'And do not call anyone on earth "father", for you have one Father, and he is in heaven.'[8]

In the Body of Christ, each of us is both a learner and a teacher whether consciously so or not. We may think we do all the receiving and none of the giving, or vice versa. But a relationship of brothers and sisters is two-way.

In recent years more and more churches have seen the need for Christians to see themselves as the Body of Christ functioning on earth. As Christians begin to relate more with one another in the way God intended, we should see more and more how re-parenting can heal our self-images.

Building a better self-image

13

Read Ephesians 4:11–16, preferably in the Living Bible.

Have you discovered the part or parts you play in the Body of

Christi? _____ What part do you see yourself having in

the Body? _____

_____

Are you involved enough in a local part of the Body of Christ

to begin to see how you fit into it? _____

Ask God to show you your place in the church. Make sure you are
worshipping and working with other Christians.

14

Moving Towards His Image

As you launch into a new venture with God to improve your self-image and carry you further down the path of becoming in the image of Christ, remember that your self-image is tied closely to your self-respect. Your behaviour and attitudes become very important to restructuring and maintaining your self-image.

The choices you make and the consequences of those choices have a profound effect on your self-image. If you choose to violate personal and Christian standards, you lose respect for yourself and undermine your self-esteem. With loss of self-respect often comes a loss of confidence in your ability to do what you know is right. Your self-image erodes with each choice you make that violates your beliefs and personal values.

Today Christians do not feel so constrained to live within the same narrow, specific limits as did many Christians a few decades ago. This, however, makes it more difficult for us to find the limits we should recognize. When secular society dismissed Judeo-Christian standards of ethics and morality, one principle it adopted was this: 'If it feels good, do it!' More thoughtful persons realized that society couldn't survive by that principle alone, however, so a limitation was attached: 'If it doesn't hurt anybody else, it's OK!' Modern Christians cannot please God if they follow only those two ethical principles that serve as contemporary culture's guidelines.

Nonetheless, many people today do try to base their ethical choices on that shaky foundation, only to find that it isn't a faithful guideline. They have forgotten how deceitful the human heart is (Jer 17:9).

A system of ethics based on an individual's feelings and rational abilities would be effective only if his or her basic nature could be trusted to be always loving and fair. If that were the case, we could trust that person's feelings and choices. But society is its own proof that human nature can't be trusted.

Modern society fails to realize that when a person's subjective feelings alone govern choices, with no objective or outside standard, there is no reason to consider ethics at all. Then each person is a law unto himself or herself, and there is no way to evaluate choices. The rightness or wrongness of a person's choice in someone else's eyes isn't even an issue.

Christians, however, know that an objective, an absolute foundation for moral and ethical standards does exist—the Word of God. When a person's choices vary from that foundation, severe consequences eventually occur. When we as Christians are faced with tough decisions, we have some absolutes to guide us towards making the best decision for everyone, now and later, without colouring the situation totally with our own immediate desires.

Yet not every right choice is easy to discern. Christians might like every decision to be spelled out in the Bible as either right or wrong, but there is a grey area for many of the decisions we must make. In this grey area we make many decisions that affect our self-image. Any time we choose to conduct ourselves in a manner that we cannot respect, we undermine our self-esteem, sense of worth, and self-confidence.

The goal of Christian living

The basic principle for all our conduct as Christians was expressed by Paul in his letter to the Colossians, 'And whatever you do, whether in word or deed, do it all in the name of the Lord Jesus, giving thanks to God the Father through him.'[1]

Many Christians seem to have changed that verse so that it reads, 'Do many things in the name of the Lord Jesus Christ.' At least, this is the way they live their lives. As Christians, however, we should have a definite goal to bring glory and honour to God through our lives in *all* we do. All our behaviour should be aimed at showing forth God's righteousness which, as discussed previously, He has already put within us.

To do this, we must know what God calls right and wrong. We need 'the mind of Christ' if we are to apply scriptural admonitions to life's circumstances. We can't depend on learning godly values in today's secular society —or even from our parents unless they themselves were thoroughly grounded in Scripture. By itself, we can't even depend on 'the still small voice' of the Holy Spirit, since we sometimes tend to override it with our own desires or 'common sense'. Certainly the daily experience of being filled with the Holy Spirit will begin to align our desires and 'common sense' outlooks on life with those of our Lord. But the only way to be sure that is happening is to compare what the Holy Spirit seems to be saying with God's written Word as well as with the circumstances at hand.

Wrong behaviour and attitudes

Various Scripture passages clearly state what sin is. Certain behaviour and attitudes are defined as specifically wrong. Let's look, first, at one from the Old Testament that is written in the language of poetry:

> There are six things the Lord hates,
>> seven that are detestable to him:
>>> haughty eyes,
>>> a lying tongue,
>>> hands that shed innocent blood,
>>> a heart that devises wicked schemes,
>>> feet that are quick to rush into evil,
>>> a false witness who pours out lies
>>> and a man who stirs up dissension among brothers.[2]

Another is from the New Testament:

> When Christ, who is your life, appears, then you also will appear with him in glory.
>
> Put to death, therefore, whatever belongs to your earthly nature: sexual immorality, impurity, lust, evil desires and greed, which is idolatry. Because of these, the wrath of God is coming. You used to walk in these ways, in the life you once lived. But now you must rid yourselves of all such things as these: anger, rage, malice, slander, and filthy language from your lips. Do not lie to each other, since you have taken off your old self with its practices and have put on the new self, which is being renewed in knowledge in the image of its Creator.[3]

Another is also from Paul's writings:

> The acts of the sinful nature are obvious: sexual immorality, impurity and debauchery; idolatry and witchcraft; hatred, discord, jealousy, fits of rage, selfish ambition, dissensions, factions and envy; drunkenness, orgies, and the like. I warn you, as I did before, that those who live like this will not inherit the kingdom of God.[4]

In the other passages, also, particular behaviour and attitudes fit readily into the category of being wrong. Some of them are in 1 Corinthians 6:9–10 and, of course, in the

Ten Commandments found in Exodus 20:

1. You shall have no other gods before me.
2. You shall not make for yourself an idol in the form of anything in heaven above or on the earth beneath or in the waters below. You shall not bow down to them or worship them; for I, the LORD your God, am a jealous God, punishing the children for the sin of the fathers to the third and fourth generation of those who hate me, but showing love to thousands who love me and keep my commandments.
3. You shall not misuse the name of the LORD your God, for the LORD will not hold anyone guiltless who misuses his name.
4. Remember the Sabbath day by keeping it holy....
5. Honour your father and your mother, so that you may live long in the land the LORD your God is giving you.
6. You shall not murder.
7. You shall not commit adultery.
8. You shall not steal.
9. You shall not give false testimony against your neighbour.
10. You shall not covet your neighbour's house. You shall not covet your neighbour's wife, or...anything that belongs to your neighbour.[5]

Right behaviour and attitudes

Other behaviour and attitudes are clearly defined as right and good. Some examples of these are:

1. We are to share our faith with others (Mt 28:19–20).
2. We are to be kind and compassionate to one another, forgiving one another (Eph 4:32).
3. We are to give thanks in everything (1 Thess 5:18).
4. We are to think about things that are honourable and good (Phil 4:8).
5. We are to show love, joy, peace, patience, kindness,

goodness, faithfulness, gentleness and self-control—the fruit of the Spirit (Gal 5:22–23).

Maybe so, maybe not

Between specifically mentioned right and wrong behaviour, however, lies a whole range of behaviour that is not explicitly prohibited or sanctioned. These are sometimes appropriate and sometimes not. This is not an area of slightly sinful or cautiously approved behaviour, which just don't make much difference one way or the other. In fact, as we apply general principles from the Scriptures meant to be used along life's way, the specific debatable or neutral behaviour, attitude, or reaction facing us can be determined to be either right or wrong, depending on the surrounding circumstances.

As we read and study 1 Corinthians 8–10, and Romans 12–15, four principles give us guidance in how to handle choices in the debatable or neutral area as we seek to honour God and maintain personal respect in all of our behaviour. The names for these four principles are taken from *Guilt and Freedom* by Bruce Narramore and Bill Counts (Vision House, 1974).

The principle of liberty

A first general principle is the principle of liberty. Two verses Paul gave us state this clearly: 'Eat anything sold in the meat market' [which in those days sold meat that had been offered as sacrifices to idols] 'without raising questions of conscience, for, "The earth is the Lord's, and everything in it,"'[6] and 'As one who is in the Lord Jesus, I am fully convinced that no food is unclean in itself. But if anyone regards something as unclean, then for him it is unclean.'[7]

The emphasis in these passages is on freedom, but it is freedom to choose: '"Everything is permissible for me"—

but I will not be mastered by anything.'⁸ Keeping this in mind, we then ask, 'Am I likely to become enslaved to this behaviour or attitude?' Some activities may not be physically addicting but they can create an emotional dependence. Some of us may become enslaved to hobbies or favourite activities that keep us from growing in our lives in other ways. Some of us even become enslaved to our daydreams and imaginations.

The principle of expediency or helpfulness

A second principle is based on the verse just referred to: '"Everything is permissible for me"—but not everything is beneficial.'⁹ Although we are permitted to engage in a wide range of activities, if we find they are not helpful to us, we should restrain from those activities. We should ask ourselves, Is this behaviour beneficial or profitable? Does it move me towards the goal of becoming like Christ? Does it make me a better person?

Of course this doesn't mean we can't relax, have fun and enjoy ourselves. There are many beneficial and profitable activities besides Bible study, prayer, evangelism and Christian meetings. Some Christians feel guilty if they aren't doing something they regard as 'spiritual' all the time. They tend to look down on others who don't feel the same way.

One of the benefits of a healthy self-image is the ability to relax and have fun, yet maintain a balance in life. It's OK with God for us to have a good time. In fact it aids physical, emotional and spiritual health.

The principle of love and consideration

A third principle is also stated by Paul:

> But if anyone says to you, "This has been offered in sacrifice," then do not eat it, both for the sake of the man who told you

and for conscience' sake—the other man's conscience, I mean, not yours. For why should my freedom be judged by another's conscience? If I take part in the meal with thankfulness, why am I denounced because of something I thank God for?

So whether you eat or drink or whatever you do, do it all for the glory of God. Do not cause anyone to stumble, whether Jews, Greeks or the church of God—even as I try to please everybody in every way. For I am not seeking my own good but the good of many, so that they may be saved. Follow my example, as I follow the example of Christ.[10]

This principle of love and consideration for others deals with the impact our behaviour will have on someone else. Paul had introduced this principle a little earlier in his discussion: '"Everything is permissible"—but not everything is constructive.'[11]

So we ask, Is this behaviour constructive or edifying to others? Will this activity help or hinder other persons in their Christian lives, or non-Christians in coming nearer to accepting Christ?

Again, it's important to note that Paul isn't saying we should engage only in activities that are specifically spiritual or ministerial in nature. We see as we study the Scriptures that balance is the key to a healthy self-image. A person can keep going in even a good direction too long and thus become unbalanced in his or her Christian life.

Using this principle and the verse given above, however, we Christians often fall into two traps. First is the problem of being too concerned about what people will think. Paul points out a distinction we must make: 'We are not trying to please men but God, who tests our hearts.'[12] Pleasing God does not always please everybody else.

Second is the problem of adopting an across-the-board rule where the Bible doesn't state one. It may seem much easier to have a firm rule to cover all contingencies in some broad area, rather than having to take time and effort to consider choices whenever something in that area comes up.

The fallacy of that second type of thinking becomes evident when we apply it to such everyday practices as dressing, eating and drinking. Knowing that whatever we wear, eat or drink will always offend at least one person somewhere, it would be foolish to say, 'Just to be on the safe side, I will never wear, eat or drink anything.' Adopting such a rule even in areas that are harder to discern is the beginning of *legalism* (which is the basing of our acceptance to other people or to God on our performance). Paul's counsel in 1 Corinthians 10:28–33 really says, If you know it will offend the people you are with, then don't do it; if it won't, then it's OK.

Some immature people insist on using their freedom without concern for other people they're with. To do that is not freedom in Christ but simple selfishness, a violation of the principle of love and consideration. Then there are Christians who try to set universal Christian rules that are based not so much on Scripture as on assumptions about Scripture and on their own cultural practices.

One such situation arose when many young men during the sixties grew long hair and beards. If you were old enough, you will recall how that practice was condemned by many parental and biblical authorities as being wrong and unbiblical. All the while, pictures of Jesus with long hair and a beard hung on the walls of their homes and churches.

Here is an interesting example of a practice that itself wasn't unbiblical or harmful. For many young men, of course, growing long hair and beards was a sign of rebellion or of giving up, not only on authority but on the world in general. Such young men needed help not in getting their hair cut but in sorting out their views of themselves and the world. Other young men grew their hair long just because it was popular among their peers.

Discerning adults tried to probe the differences between those two underlying reasons for the custom and then talk out the differing feelings and viewpoints about what it meant. In this instance, the principles of liberty, expediency or helpfulness, and of enslavement (to the attitudes of the counter-culture around them) needed to be considered in each individual's case.

To make an absolute rule about some behaviour that is not an absolute in Scripture is a violation of biblical principles. We need to be careful to distinguish between our culture and scriptural revelation.

The principle of faith

A fourth principle to consider in making choices is the principle of faith. 'But the man who has doubts is condemned if he eats, because his eating is not from faith; and everything that does not come from faith is sin.'[13]

We must be convinced in our own minds, before God, that what we are doing is OK. Some of us were taught that certain things were wrong. As a result, when we take part in those activities we feel guilty and condemn ourselves. Paul is saying that such activities are sin for us, even though they are not explicitly defined that way in Scripture. We hinder our walk with the Lord when we engage in an activity that causes us to condemn ourselves.

The issue here is maturity and biblical understanding. It hits right at the heart of the parenting and re-parenting processes. As we grow and wholeheartedly accept God's true standards instead of those of our childhood, which we may have assumed or were told were God's standards, we may be able later to take part in those activities without sinning. In such cases, of course, we would still keep in mind the other principles discussed previously. On the other hand, the more we mature, the more we may realize that activities we once saw as harmless may not be as beneficial or edifying as ones we would like our present lives to include.

Check-list for choices

We can summarize the use of these principles as follows:

1. Be fully convinced in your own mind that an activity is OK for you and that you can engage in it by faith.

2. Know the people you are with and don't engage in any activity that would cause them unnecessary problems. Don't insist on your own way regardless of who you're with.

3. Don't engage in any activity forbidden in the Bible. However, if you do, remember that God understands and is patient with your lack of perfection. The apostle John stated, 'But if anybody does sin, we have one who speaks to the Father in our defence—Jesus Christ, the Righteous One.'[14] Agree with God that it was wrong and accept His forgiveness and cleansing, which is offered to you continually. This is the emphasis of 1 John 1:9, 'If we confess our sins, he is faithful and just and will forgive us our sins and purify us from all unrighteousness.

4. Don't continue to do anything you know is of no value to you and your growth in Christ. Don't participate in anything that could become addicting or a destructive habit.

> *Remember that you are free*
> *to be the divine original that*
> *God created you to be.*

People with healthy self-images are relaxed about their behaviour. They know their personal boundaries and thus are not fearful of the choices they will face each day.

Remember that you are free to be the divine original that God created you to be. Enjoy your freedom and use it as an opportunity to grow and become more like Christ, expressing more and more the image of God.

Building a better self-image

14

You are created in God's image. Genesis 1:26–27 says, 'Then God said, "Let us make man in our image, in our likeness...." So God created man in his own image, in the image of God he created him; male and female he created them.'

According to these verses, you are created in the _____

and _____ of God.

List five ways you see the image of God in you and other people.

_____

_____

_____

_____

_____

According to Genesis 1:31, 'God saw all that he had made, and it was very good.' Since He made you, does this mean that you

are good? _____

To be created in God's image means that you are a reflection or an imprint of God. As a footprint on a muddy road is an imprint of a person's shoe, so you are an imprint of God. A shoe can be placed back into its imprint; God can dwell in you as His imprint. You were created in God's image so He could dwell in you and fit comfortably in you. You are the 'temple' or dwelling place of God (1 Cor 6:19–20) and He is comfortable dwelling in you, His creation, made in His image and likeness.

15

Self-Image With a Purpose

Did you know that you are a gift to the world? If you weren't, then God would have had no reason not to take you to heaven to be with Him immediately after you trusted Christ as your Saviour and Lord. Each of us is a gift to humanity, and gifts are meant to be used. As God's gift to the world, He wants to use you to reach His world for Christ.

That means you have been given a purpose in life, which really helps in developing a healthy self-image. What is your purpose? I think it's a distinct one.

An executive hirer, a 'head-hunter' who goes out and hires corporation executives for other firms, once told me, 'When I get an executive that I'm trying to hire for someone else, I like to disarm him. I offer him a drink, take my coat off, then my waistcoat, undo my tie, put my feet up and talk about baseball, football, family, whatever, until he's all relaxed. Then, when I think I've got him relaxed, I lean over, look him squarely in the eye and say, "What's your purpose in life?" It's amazing how top executives fall apart at that question.

'Well, I was interviewing this fellow the other day, had him all disarmed, with my feet up on his desk, talking about football. Then I leant over and said, "What's your purpose in life, Bob?" And he said, without blinking an eye, "To go

to heaven and take as many people with me as I can." For
the first time in my career I was speechless.'

That others might know

A result to be expected from developing a healthy self-
image as a Christian is the desire to become part of God's
redemptive plan. When you see humankind as God does,
and grasp the fact that He created every person in His
image and that Jesus died for each of them, your desire
increases to share God's love with those 'for whom Christ
died.'[1]

Now you may not think that many or any people have
come to Christ directly through your telling them about
Him, but perhaps more are on their way as a result of your
life than you may know.

The way you live your life should point to something
different from the normal life about you. If as a Christian
you believe in yourself, it will—whether or not you realize
it. But, as mentioned previously, that kind of *living witness*
needs to be accompanied by a *telling witness*. If one or the
other of those witnesses hasn't been dominant in your life,
an improved self-image is likely to make a difference.

Witnessing and self-esteem

Even without a healthy self-image, our Christian training
has made us realize that we ought to share Christ with
others. For those without a healthy self-image, that
imperative has brought only a sense of guilt when years
passed without seeing anyone come to Christ through them.
In fact it has compounded their poor image of themselves.

Many people believe that their lives aren't good enough
to witness verbally for Jesus. Some are afraid of possible
negative reactions to their efforts to tell others about Him.
Others think they will bungle any attempts to share the

gospel, leaving hearers only more confused. Some people fear all three of those possibilities.

Let's look at those fears a little more closely and see if they fit in with the three pillars of self-image we've been discussing. To recognize that you do belong and are loved, that you are worthy and that you are competent through the Holy Spirit, is going to make those excuses look a lot less formidable.

> *The more we see ourselves as God sees us, the more we realize the need for all people to be made aware that God loves them.*

The more we see ourselves as God sees us—accepted by God, loved, forgiven, made in His image—the more we realize the need for all people to be made aware that God loves them. They need to know that He 'made him who had no sin to be sin for us, so that in him we might become the righteousness of God.'[2]

When you do share your faith, letting God take care of the outcome, your self-image will soar even further.

A counsellor friend of mine told me about an experience he had recently. After Connor, a young dentist, left the counselling office, my friend felt a sense of exhilaration that he had to share with someone. He bounded up the stairs and announced to the office staff that Connor had just prayed with him to receive Christ. Through my friend's witness, this young dentist, who had been extremely depressed when he first came for counselling, had accepted Jesus' death on the Cross as payment for his sins. As a result, my friend's sense of worth was confirmed anew because he was participating with God in His ministry 'to seek and to save the lost.'[3]

Sharing your faith is part of improving your self-image, and improving your self-image is part of discovering the desire, drive and competence to share your faith.

Realize too that your part in other people's sharing of the gospel is another reason for your being on this earth. Being an active part of the Body of Christ, contributing yourself, your talents and your income so that the Body of Christ as a whole will have a better witness to the world, are all meaningful parts of your purpose for being here, even if you can't see specific ways in which your part in the whole is all that evident.

When my friend ran upstairs to tell the people in his office about Connor receiving Christ, they were as excited as he. They knew that in some way they too had a part in Connor's finding new life in Christ.

A person committed to any ideal is a significant force in society. Such commitment should give that individual a sense of personal worth, a sense that his or her life will leave a mark in eternity. The joy of evangelism is a powerful antidote for feelings of insignificance and unworthiness. People who share their faith in Christ can find vital and permanent significance in knowing that their lives count in humanity's most noble and crucial cause.

Fat Albert

It's like Doug Vinson's chronicle of 'Fat Albert':

"See Fat Albert, the world's fattest man," blared the pre-recorded sales pitch. "He is real and he is alive and he weighs 870 pounds!"

I walked up the platform's well-worn steps half-expecting "Fat Albert" to be a stuffed doll or some other deception. I was truly surprised as I peered behind the three-sided partition and saw an enormous man sitting on a small seat. . . .

Fat Albert said he was born in a small town in Mississippi. A genetic defect caused him to accumulate his abnormal weight and yes, indeed, he did weigh 870 pounds.

I stepped to the side as other people came into the booth.... He patiently answered their questions and had a ready, humorous reply for the taunts a scoffer hurled.

I was about to leave when one of the teenagers in the group asked him how he felt being the world's fattest man.

"Well, we're all made in God's image, aren't we?" Albert said. "And we all come in different shapes and sizes. God made me the way I am for a purpose and He made you the way you are for a purpose. The Bible says that the body is going to die and the spirit is going to live on, so it is more important how we live than how we look."

As others came in, he described how he became a Christian when he was sixteen. In the process, in a warm, low-key manner, he presented God's plan of salvation. Some stood blank-faced, but most listened politely.

Stepping closer, I noticed a sticker on the wall behind him: "Life is God's Gift—Fight Abortion."[4]

One of a kind

No one else in the world is like you. Now you may think that some people would say, 'Thank God for that!' And that's OK—because you can say that too! You can thank God that out of four and a half thousand million people alive today, there's no one like you. Your prayer can be: God, I want to be, with all my uniqueness, what you created me to be. I don't want to be like someone else. I just want to be myself in all that you created me to be, not to glorify myself but to glorify you.

After hearing me present a message on forgiveness as it relates to a healthy self-image, a college student, Byron Michow, wrote this psalm and titled it 'Me'. It describes beautifully the lifetime struggle many of us have trying to be like others:

All my life I've tried
    to please others.
All my life I've put
    on an act for others.
I will not
    do this.
For if I spend my time
    trying to be someone else,
Who will spend the time being me?

If there is no one else like you, why do you want to be like someone else? My desire for you is that you will not desire to be like someone else, but like *the unique you* God created you to be.

You are the best *you* there ever will be. Not since creation nor till the end of time will there be another just like you. That means that in being yourself, you don't have to be in competition with anyone.

Your singularity isn't a basis for pride but for praise to God. 'I praise you because I am fearfully and wonderfully made; your works are wonderful.'[5]

Writing on the subject of self-esteem, Christian psychologist Bruce Narramore recognizes the relationship between our uniqueness and self-esteem relative to serving:

> Just as God used different people with different gifts throughout the Bible. He is using each of us today in a special way. We have all been created with a unique personality and with talents, and we must recognize that our uniqueness to God is a source of self-esteem. We have each been chosen to fulfill an aspect of His ministry, and so we do not need to compete with others around us to prove our worth.[6]

Doing good

Part of our purpose in this world is to do good to others. Throughout the Scriptures we are admonished to please others (our 'neighbour') for their good, to build them up (Rom 15:2), to 'do good to all people, especially to those who belong to the family of believers'[17] never to 'tire of doing what is right'[8] and 'not become weary in doing good.'[9]

When our actions do result in good for others, coinciding with who we truly are in Christ, it reinforces positive feelings and attitudes we have about ourselves.

Ask yourself, 'When was the last time I felt especially good about myself?' Was it when you had done something good for someone? If so, God intended it that way. You experienced the truth of this biblical principle: We were created to do good to one another. The condition that interferes with that is humanity's fall into sin.

Doing our best

Another factor that will affect our self-image is whether or not we do our best in situations that are important to God, others and ourselves. Paul admonished the Galatians: 'Let everyone be sure that he is doing his very best, for he will have the personal satisfaction of work well done, and won't need to compare himself with someone else.'[10]

Desiring to do your best is not the same as wanting to be the best at something. To want to be the best can be motivated by the desire to be accepted by others (or even by the desire to accept yourself). To desire to be the best requires comparing yourself to others. In that case either you or another person—whoever is not the best—must be discounted in some way in order to establish the importance of the person who turns out to be the best at some effort.

When you do your best, you like yourself. By that I don't mean doing your best in order to please others, but doing your best in order to be all that God created you to be to His glory. If you do your best, with the gifts, talents and abilities God has given you, in the power of the Holy Spirit, you needn't care if hundreds of people are better than you. You can still look in the mirror and say, 'I like you, and so does God.'

Thank you, God, for me

David, the Psalmist, had a healthy self-image. Here is a psalm of praise he wrote about the omnipresence (infinite presence), omniscience (infinite knowledge) and sovereignty (supreme authority) of God over all aspects of life:

O LORD, you have searched me
  and you know me.
You know when I sit and when I rise;
  you perceive my thoughts from afar.
You discern my going out and my lying down;
  you are familiar with all my ways.
Before a word is on my tongue
  you know it completely, O LORD.
You hem me in, behind and before;
  you have laid your hand upon me.
Such knowledge is too wonderful for me,
  too lofty for me to attain.

Where can I go from your Spirit?
  Where can I flee from your presence?
If I go up to the heavens, you are there;
  if I make my bed in the depths, you are there.
If I rise on the wings of the dawn,
  if I settle on the far side of the sea,
even there your hand will guide me,
  your right hand will hold me fast. . . .

For you created my inmost being;
  you knit me together in my mother's womb.
I praise you because I am fearfully and wonderfully made;
  your works are wonderful,
  I know that full well.

My frame was not hidden from you
   when I was made in the secret place.
When I was woven together in the depths of the earth,
   your eyes saw my unformed body.
All the days ordained for me
   were written in your book
   before one of them came to me.
How precious to me [or *concerning* me] are your thoughts,
      O God![11]

How often, instead of praise, have you heard the complaint from yourself or another Christian, 'Well, Mother Nature sure messed me up when she got to my nose [or hair, or body, or brain].' Notice that David praised God for the way He made him: 'I will give thanks to You for I have been awesomely and wonderfully made.' As Christians we need daily to express a similar attitude.

What? Roses for me?

A healthy self-image shows itself in other ways too. I boarded a plane in Atlanta one day and saw something I hadn't seen before. To get back to the section with the cheapest seats I had to go through the first class section. A stewardess was standing there saying, 'Welcome, thanks for flying with us,' while holding a dozen roses. Now I've flown close to five thousand flights (I count every one of them), but I had never seen a stewardess with her arms full of flowers.

I said to her, 'Oh, your boyfriend bought you some flowers?'

'No,' she said.

Then I asked, 'Your hubby did?'

'No.'

'Well, then,' I continued, 'who did?'

'I did,' she said. Now that was strange.

So I went and put my things in my seat, came back,

introduced myself, found out she was a Christian and said, 'Could I ask you a personal question?'

'Sure,' she replied.

'Why did you buy yourself a dozen roses?'

She responded, 'Because I like myself.'

Think of that. Because she liked herself she went out and bought herself a dozen roses.

A room full of flowers

If ever I have a lonely night away from home, missing my family, it's New Year's Eve. For thirteen years I've spent that night away from Dottie and my children in the same motel room in Laguna Beach, California.

Each year shortly after Christmas I make a speaker's circuit of six or seven student conferences for six days. I start out on the US East Coast, where my family and I spend Christmas with Dottie's folks. Then, after a week of travelling and speaking night and day, I end up on the West Coast on New Year's Eve and I head to Laguna Beach. My family is still in New England, and I am emotionally, physically and spiritually drained.

Last year I flew into Orange County Airport and was picked up by my friend Don Stewart, with whom I've written several books. As we drove through Laguna Canyon we passed a couple who were selling flowers from their lorry.

'Stop!' I said to Don. I got out of the car and bought five dozen flowers. Picture, if you can, trying to open the door of a Honda Civic and climbing in while holding five dozen flowers. It isn't easy.

Don didn't comment on the fact that he now had a car full of flowers, but you could tell he was puzzled. I knew he was trying to figure it out. Here his close and dear friend was buying five dozen flowers and heading for a motel room, alone, in Laguna Beach. 'Just what's going on here?' were the words I was sure he was thinking. 'Josh McDowell, Christian speaker and author, staff member of Campus Crusade for Christ, whose wife and three children are in Boston, is going to a motel room on New Year's Eve with five dozen flowers. Is he really the person I think he is?'

After travelling past several more blocks in silence, Don finally blurted out, 'Why all the flowers?' Enthusiastically I told him the story of the airline stewardess and her roses, as well as some of the points related in this book.

Then I concluded, 'These flowers are reminders to me of who God is, what Jesus had done for me, and who I am, by God's grace. Tonight I'm going to put these flowers all over that room as a reminder that God loves me, cares for me and forgives me, and that I can like and accept myself, while being thankful to be used by Him to share His love with the world, even though I'll be spending New Year's Eve in a motel room alone.'

Maybe the time has come for you to go out and buy yourself a dozen roses.

Or maybe you need to say simply, 'Thank you, God, for who I am. Thank you for my strong points and for my weaknesses. I want to yield my limitations to you to make me a better instrument to share your love with the world. Lord, I want to love the world and I need to start by loving and accepting myself.'

Building
a better self-image

I5

You are special because you have been created by God for a special purpose. We find portions of His purpose throughout His Word.

Genesis 1:27–28: '...male and female he created them. God blessed them and said to them, "Be fruitful and increase in number; fill the earth and subdue it. Rule over the fish of the sea and the birds of the air and over every living creature that moves on the ground."' To whom did God give this command?

_____

1 Thessalonians 2:4: 'We speak as men approved by God to be entrusted with the gospel.' For what purpose have you

been approved? _____

2 Corinthians 5:20: 'We are...Christ's ambassadors, as though God were making his appeal through us.'

Whose ambassador are you? _____

Being Christ's ambassador means appealing to people to receive Christ as Saviour; it also includes every one of our actions. Ephesians 2:10 (LB) says, 'It is God himself who has made us what we are and given us new lives from Christ Jesus; and long ages ago he planned that we should spend these lives in helping others.' What did God plan for us to do as Christians?

_____

_____

Postscript

Habits to enhance your self-image

1. Do not label yourself negatively ('I am clumsy' and so on). You tend to become the label you give yourself.
2. Behave assertively (but not aggressively) even in threatening situations, particularly when you don't feel like doing so.
3. When you fail, admit or confess it to God, your Father, and then refuse to condemn yourself. 'Therefore, there is now no condemnation for those who are in Christ Jesus' (Rom 8:1). Remember, you are in the process of becoming like Christ. Growth takes time. Be as kind to yourself as you would be (or would hope to be) to any other person.
4. Do not compare yourself with others. You are a unique person. God enjoys you in your uniqueness; have a similar attitude towards yourself.
5. Concentrate and meditate on God's grace, love and acceptance—not on criticisms from other people.
6. Associate with friends who are positive, who delight in you and who enjoy life.
7. Start helping others to see themselves as God sees them... by accepting them, loving them, and encouraging them. Give them the dignity they deserve as one of God's unique human creatures.

8. Learn to laugh; look for the humour in life and experience it.

9. Have expectations of others which are realistic, taking into account each person's specific talents, gifts, abilities and potential.

10. Relax and take it easy. If the sinless Jesus waited in preparation thirty years for a three-year ministry, perhaps God isn't in as much of a hurry with you as you may suppose He is.

11. Do what is right and pleasing in the eyes of God. When our lives reflect God's character, we are a lot happier and it affects our attitude about ourselves.

12. Be positive (Phil 4:8). See how long you can go without saying something negative about another person or situation.

13. Lead others with influence and wise guidance rather than with autocratic power.

14. Love in accordance with God's model of *agape* love and balance love with limits.

If you learn to practise the principles in this book, and in this Postscript in particular, some day you may be writing a letter similar to this one I received from Marilyn:

Dear Josh,

I had a lot of rage and hurts in me that stemmed from unforgiveness towards God and my parents for the way I turned out. Summed up, I didn't like myself and felt it hard to accept who I am. The Lord knew I needed to hear your message on self-image.

Thank you. I'm beginning to see myself as God sees me. This is the start of a long-awaited healing.

Marilyn

In Philippians 3:13–14 (RSV), Paul says to Marilyn and to you, 'Forgetting what lies behind and straining forward to what lies ahead,... press on toward the goal for the prize of the upward call of God in Christ Jesus.'

Notes

Chapter One
1. John De Vines, *How Much Are You Worth?*, Grand Rapids, Michigan: Bibles for India, n.d., pp.3-4

Chapter Two
1. Phil 2:3–5   2. Rom 12:3 (NASB)
3. Col 3:1–4, 10   4. Phil 4:8
5. Earl D. Radmacher, *You & Your Thoughts,* Palm Springs, California: Ronald N. Haynes Publishers, Inc., 1982, pp.10-11
6. 1 Cor 15:10   7. Gal 6:4
8. Rollo May, *Man's Search for Himself,* New York: W. W. Norton and Co., Inc., 1953, p.100
9. Walter Bauer, *A Greek-English Lexicon of the New Testament,* trans., William F. Arndt and F. Wilbur Gingrich, Chicago: University of Chicago Press, 1957, p.874
10. 2 Cor 10:12 (NASB)   11. Ps 8:5 (AV)   12. 1 Pet 5:5; Jas 4:6
13. Prov 16:18   14. 1 Cor 15:57   15. Rom 8:37 (PHILLIPS)
16. Elizabeth Skoglund, *The Whole Christian,* New York: Harper & Row, 1976
17. Eph 5:28–29

Chapter Four
1. W. Hugh Missildine, *Your Inner Child of the Past,* New York: Simon and Schuster, 1963, pp.37-39

Chapter Five

1. W. Hugh Missildine, *Your Inner Child of the Past,* New York: Simon and Schuster, 1963, p.82
2. Cecil Osborne, *The Art of Understanding Yourself,* Grand Rapids, Michigan: Zondervan Publishing House, 1967, p.148
3. Stanley Coopersmith, *The Antecedents of Self-Esteem,* San Francisco: W. H. Freeman, 1967, p.165
4. Gal 4:19   5. Eph 4:13   6. Eph 4:15   7. Col 1:22
8. Col 1:28   9. Gal 5:22–23

Chapter Six

1. 2 Cor 1:3–4   2. Phil 1:6

Chapter Seven

1. Max Lerner, 'The Vanishing American Father,' *McCall's,* May 1965, p.95.
2. Paul Popenoe, 'Why Are Fathers Failures?' Publ. 206, The American Institute of Family Relations, 5287 Sunset Blvd., Los Angeles, CA 90027, n.d.
3. Harold M. Voth, *The Castrated Family,* Mission, Kansas: Sheed Andrews & McMeel, Inc., 1977, pp.4-5
4. Herb Goldberg, *The Hazards of Being Male,* Signet, New American Library, 1977
5. Arthur Janov, *The Primal Scream,* Delta, Dell, 1971

Chapter Eight

1. These concepts are developed in detail by Maurice Wagner, *The Sensation of Being Somebody,* Grand Rapids, Michigan: Zondervan Publishing House, 1975, pp.32-37
2. James D. Mallory and Stanley C. Baldwin, *The Kink and I,* Grand Rapids, Michigan: Zondervan Publishing House, 1965, p.83

Chapter Nine

1. 2 Cor 5:17
2. Most of these are taken from Linda Raney Wright, *Staying On Top When Things Go Wrong,* Wheaton, Illinois: Tyndale House, 1983
3. 1 Cor 12:13

Chapter Ten
1. 1 Jn 4:10   2. Jn 15:9   3. Jn 17:9–11, 22–23
4. Jn 3:16   5. Rom 5:8   6. Jn 16:27   7. Rom 8:38–39
8. Ps 50:21 (NASB)   9. Eph 2:8–9   10. Jn 1:12
11. *Campus Life,* January 1980
12. Rom 15:7   13. 1 Jn 3:1   14. Jn 14:11
15. Jn 14:20   16. 1 Cor 12:13, 24–27

Chapter Eleven
1. 1 Jn 1:9   2. Col 2:13–14   3. 1 Pet 1:18–19
4. Ps 32:5   5. Rom 8:1   6. Ps 103:10–13
7. Mt 5:23–24   8. Heb 10:17   9. 1 Cor 2:16
10. Eph 4:32   11. Jer 17:9 (AV)   12. Rom 3:23
13. 1 Jn 1:8 (RSV)   14. Judg 20:16   15. Gen 1:26
16. 1 Cor 11:7   17. Mt 6:26; 10:31   18. Mt 12:11–12
19. 2 Cor 5:21 (LB). This paraphrase communicates in a more
    powerful way the emotional intent of the verse.

Chapter Twelve
1. Acts 1:8 (NASB)   2. Mt 5:6 (NASB)   3. Rom 12:1 (LB)
4. 1 Jn 1:9 (LB)   5. Eph 5:18   6. 1 Jn 5:14–15
7. Phil 4:13   8. 2 Cor 3:5   9. Phil 1:6

Chapter Thirteen
1. Acts 2:42–45
2. These ideas are discussed in Gene Getz, *Sharpening the Focus
   of the Church,* Moody Press, 1974
3. Acts 2:46–47   4. 1 Pet 2:2–3
5. Eph 4:11–15   6. Jn 14:9–10
7. Ps 139:23–24 (NASB)   8. Mt 23:9

Chapter Fourteen
1. Col 3:17   2. Prov 6:16–19   3. Col 3:4–9
4. Gal 5:19–21   5. Ex 20:3–17   6. 1 Cor 10:25–26
7. Rom 14:14   8. 1 Cor 6:12b   9. 1 Cor 6:12a
10. 1 Cor 10:28—11:1   11. 1 Cor 10:23b   12. 1 Thess 2:4
13. Rom 14:23   14. 1 Jn 2:1

Chapter Fifteen
1. Rom 14:15   2. 2 Cor 5:21   3. Lk 19:10 (GNB)
4. *Moody Monthly,* July/August 1981, p.25
5. Ps 139:14
6. Bruce Narramore, *You're Someone Special,* Grand Rapids, Michigan: Zondervan Publishing House, 1978, p.41
7. Gal 6:10   8. 2 Thess 3:13   9. Gal 6:9
10. Gal 6:4 (LB)   11. Ps 139:1–10, 13–17

Have You Heard of the

Four Spiritual Laws?

Just as there are physical laws that govern the physical universe, so are there spiritual laws which govern your relationship with God.

LAW ONE

GOD **LOVES** YOU, AND OFFERS A WONDERFUL **PLAN** FOR YOUR LIFE.

(References contained in this booklet should be read in context from the Bible wherever possible.)

Written by Bill Bright. Copyright © Campus Crusade for Christ, Inc., 1965. All rights reserved.

God's Love

"For God so loved the world, that He gave His only begotten Son, that whoever believes in Him should not perish, but have eternal life" (John 3:16).

God's Plan

(Christ speaking) "I came that they might have life, and might have it abundantly" (that it might be full and meaningful) (John 10:10).

Why is it that most people are not experiencing the abundant life? Because . . .

LAW TWO

MAN IS SINFUL AND SEPARATED FROM GOD. THEREFORE, HE CANNOT KNOW AND EXPERIENCE GOD'S LOVE AND PLAN FOR HIS LIFE.

Man Is Sinful

"For all have sinned and fall short of the glory of God" (Romans 3:23).

Man was created to have fellowship with God; but, because of his stubborn self-will, he chose to go his own independent way and fellowship with God was broken. This self-will, characterized by an attitude of active rebellion or passive indifference, is evidence of what the Bible calls sin.

Man Is Separated

"For the wages of sin is death" (spiritual separation from God) (Romans 6:23).

This diagram illustrates that God is holy and man is sinful. A great gulf separates the two. The arrows illustrate that man is continually trying to reach God and the abundant life through his own efforts, such as a good life, philosophy or religion.

The third law explains the only way to bridge this gulf . . .

LAW THREE

JESUS CHRIST IS GOD'S ONLY PROVISION FOR MAN'S SIN. THROUGH HIM YOU CAN KNOW AND EXPERIENCE GOD'S LOVE AND PLAN FOR YOUR LIFE.

He Died in Our Place

"But God demonstrates His own love toward us, in that while we were yet sinners, Christ died for us" (Romans 5:8).

He Rose from the Dead

"Christ died for our sins . . . He was buried . . . He was raised on the third day, according to the Scriptures . . . He appeared to Peter, then to the twelve. After that He appeared to more than five hundred . . ." (I Corinthians 15:3-6).

He Is the Only Way to God

"Jesus said to him, 'I am the way, and the truth, and the life; no one comes to the Father, but through Me'" (John 14:6).

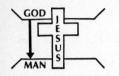

This diagram illustrates that God has bridged the gulf which separates us from Him by sending His Son, Jesus Christ, to die on the cross in our place to pay the penalty for our sins.

It is not enough just to know these three laws . . .

LAW FOUR

WE MUST INDIVIDUALLY **RECEIVE** JESUS CHRIST AS SAVIOR AND LORD; THEN WE CAN KNOW AND EXPERIENCE GOD'S LOVE AND PLAN FOR OUR LIVES.

We Must Receive Christ

"But as many as received Him, to them He gave the right to become children of God, even to those who believe in His name" (John 1:12).

We Receive Christ Through Faith

"For by grace you have been saved through faith; and that not of yourselves, it is the gift of God; not as a result of works, that no one should boast" (Ephesians 2:8,9).

When We Receive Christ, We Experience a New Birth.

(Read John 3:1-8.)

We Receive Christ by Personal Invitation

(Christ is speaking): "Behold, I stand at the door and knock; if any one hears My voice and opens the door, I will come in to him" (Revelation 3:20).

Receiving Christ involves turning to God from self (repentance) and trusting Christ to come into our lives to forgive our sins and to make us the kind of people He wants us to be. Just to agree intellectually that Jesus Christ is the Son of God and that He died on the cross for our sins is not enough. Nor is it enough to have an emotional experience. We receive Jesus Christ by faith, as an act of the will.

These two circles represent two kinds of lives:

SELF-DIRECTED LIFE
S — Self is on the throne
† — Christ is outside the life
● — Interests are directed by self, often resulting in discord and frustration

CHRIST-DIRECTED LIFE
† — Christ is in the life and on the throne
S — Self is yielding to Christ
● — Interests are directed by Christ, resulting in harmony with God's plan

Which circle best represents your life?

Which circle would you like to have represent your life?

The following explains how you can receive Christ:

YOU CAN RECEIVE CHRIST RIGHT NOW BY FAITH THROUGH PRAYER

(Prayer is talking with God)

God knows your heart and is not so concerned with your words as He is with the attitude of your heart. The following is a suggested prayer:

"Lord Jesus, I need You. Thank You for dying on the cross for my sins. I open the door of my life and receive You as my Savior and Lord. Thank You for forgiving my sins and giving me eternal life. Take control of the throne of my life. Make me the kind of person You want me to be."

Does this prayer express the desire of your heart?

If it does, pray this prayer right now, and Christ will come into your life, as He promised.

How to Know That Christ Is in Your Life

Did you receive Christ into your life? According to His promise in Revelation 3:20, where is Christ right now in relation to you? Christ said that He would come into your life. Would He mislead you? On what authority do you know that God has answered your prayer? (The trustworthiness of God Himself and His Word.)

The Bible Promises Eternal Life to All Who Receive Christ

"And the witness is this, that God has given us eternal life, and this life is in His Son. He who has the Son has the life; he who does not have the Son of God does not have the life. These things I have written to you who believe in the name of the Son of God, in order that you may know that you have eternal life" (I John 5:11-13).

Thank God often that Christ is in your life and that He will never leave you (Hebrews 13:5). You can know on the basis of His promise that Christ lives in you and that you have eternal life, from the very moment you invite Him in. He will not deceive you.

An important reminder . . .

DO NOT DEPEND UPON FEELINGS

The promise of God's Word, the Bible — not our feelings — is our authority. The Christian lives by faith (trust) in the trustworthiness of God Himself and His Word. This train diagram illustrates the relationship between **fact** (God and His Word), **faith** (our trust in God and His Word), and **feeling** (the result of our faith and obedience) (John 14:21).

The train will run with or without the caboose. However, it would be useless to attempt to pull the train by the caboose. In the same way, we, as Christians, do not depend on feelings or emotions, but we place our faith (trust) in the trustworthiness of God and the promises of His Word.

NOW THAT YOU HAVE RECEIVED CHRIST

The moment that you received Christ by faith, as an act of the will, many things happened, including the following:

I. Christ came into your life (Revelation 3:20 and Colossians 1:27).
2. Your sins were forgiven (Colossians 1:14).
3. You became a child of God (John 1:12).
4. You received eternal life (John 5:24).
5. You began the great adventure for which God created you (John 10:10; II Corinthians 5:17 and I Thessalonians 5:18).

Can you think of anything more wonderful that could happen to you than receiving Christ? Would you like to thank God in prayer right now for what He has done for you? By thanking God, you demonstrate your faith.

To enjoy your new life
to the fullest . . .

SUGGESTIONS FOR CHRISTIAN GROWTH

Spiritual growth results from trusting Jesus Christ. "The righteous man shall live by faith" (Galatians 3:11). A life of faith will enable you to trust God increasingly with every detail of your life, and to practice the following:

G Go to God in prayer daily (John 15:7).

R Read God's Word daily (Acts 17:11)—begin with the Gospel of John.

O Obey God moment by moment (John 14:21).

W Witness for Christ by your life and words (Matthew 4:19; John 15:8).

T Trust God for every detail of your life (I Peter 5:7).

H Holy Spirit—allow Him to control and empower your daily life and witness (Galatians 5:16,17; Acts 1:8).

FELLOWSHIP IN A GOOD CHURCH

God's Word admonishes us not to forsake "the assembling of ourselves together. . ." (Hebrews 10:25). Several logs burn brightly together; but put one aside on the cold hearth and the fire goes out. So it is with your relationship to other Christians. If you do not belong to a church, do not wait to be invited. Take the initiative; call the pastor of a nearby church where Christ is honored and His Word is preached. Start this week, and make plans to attend regularly.

SPECIAL MATERIALS ARE AVAILABLE FOR CHRISTIAN GROWTH.

If you have come to know Christ personally through this presentation of the gospel, write for a free booklet especially written to assist you in your Christian growth.
A special Bible study series and an abundance of other helpful materials for Christian growth are also available. For additional information, please write Campus Crusade for Christ International, San Bernardino, CA 92414.

You will want to share this important discovery . . .

LET'S STAY -IN- TOUCH!

If you have grown personally as a result of this material, we should stay in touch. You will want to continue in your Christian growth, and to help your faith become even stronger, our team is constantly developing new materials.

We are now publishing a monthly newsletter called <u>5 Minutes with Josh</u> which will

    1) tell you about those new materials as they become available
    2) answer your tough questions
    3) give creative tips on being an effective parent
    4) let you know our ministry needs
    5) keep you up to date on my speaking schedule (so you can pray).

If you would like to receive this publication, simply fill out the coupon below and send it in. By special arrangement <u>5 Minutes with Josh</u> will come to you regularly — <u>no charge</u>.

Let's keep in touch!

Josh

☐ **Yes!** I want to receive the free subscription to **5 Minutes with JOSH**

NAME

ADDRESS

Post to Josh McDowell
c/o *5 Minutes with Josh*
Campus Crusade for Christ
103 Friar Street
Reading, Berks
England

SLC-2024